The Hummus Cookbook

100 Delicious Hummus Recipes

Table of Contents

18. Jalapeno-Cumin Combo Hummus

19. Hummus with Smoked Paprika

20. Low-Fat Yogurt Hummus

21. Cannellini Beans Hummus

22. Guacamole Hummus

23. Organic Arugula Hummus

24. Protein Rich Tofu Hummus

25. Simple Olive Hummus

26. Cashew Nuts Hummus

27. Element Rich Hummus

28. Creamy Cookie Dough Hummus

29. Italian Style Hummus

30. Two Beans Hummus

31. Fiesta Style Hummus

32. Zesty Hummus-Like Spread

33. Spicy Five Pepper Hummus

34. Sweet Potatoes Hummus

35. Sage and Oregano Hummus

36. Black Beans-Jalapeno Humus

37. Pine Nuts and Sweet Basil Hummus

38. Cauliflower Hummus

39. Wasabi Hummus

40. Cucumber with Greek Yogurt Hummus

41. Roasted Carrot Hummus

42. Black-Eyed Peas-Garlic Hummus

43. Rosemary Pumpkin and Roasted Garlic Hummus

44. Cilantro-Lime Combo Hummus

45. Pepperoncini Hummus

46. Healthy Curried Hummus

47. Hummus with Pumpkin

48. Five Spices Orange Hummus

49. Spinach Hummus

50. Edamame Hummus

51. Almond Hummus

52. Peanut Butter Hummus

53. Hot Spinach Hummus

54. Hummus with Cuban Black Beans

55. Cumin in Light Sour Cream Hummus

56. Hemp Seed Hummus

57. Pinto Beans with Wine Hummus

58. Hummus with Spiriluna Powder

59. Smoky Roasted Horseradish Hummus

60. Beetroot Hummus

61. Italian Parsley with Bland Oil Hummus

62. Hummus with Kalamata Olive

63. Coriander and Carrot Hummus

64. Yummy Dilled Hummus

65. Hummus with Chipotle Peppers

66. Hummus with Pesto Sauce

67. Hummus with Plain Yogurt and Almonds

68. Chocolate Hummus

69. Hummus with Macadamia Nuts

70. Hummus with Plain Yogurt and Cinnamon

71. Yummy Beanless Zucchini Hummus

72. Hummus with Fresh Basil

73. Healthy Raw Nut Pulp Hummus

74. Eggplant Hummus

75. Vegan Friendly Harissa Hummus

76. Hummus with Black Tea and Raspberry Jam

77. Hummus with Low Fat Sour Cream and Parmesan Cheese

78. Hummus with Chipotle Chile and Orange

79. Hummus with Tamarind and Fresh Ginger

80. Hummus with Sprouted Raw Nut

81. Hummus with Tamari and Curry Powder

82. Hummus with Wasabi

83. Tasty Broccoli Hummus94

84. Hummus with Lima Beans

85. Hummus with Sambal Oelek and Butter Beans

86. Hummus with Black Olives and Beans

87. Hummus with Serrano Peppers and Cilantro

88. Hummus with Vegetable Oil and Red Pepper Flakes

89. Green Olive, Spinach and Avocado Hummus

90. Hummus with Pine Nuts and Parsley

91. Roasted Grape Tomatoes and Garlic Hummus

92. Hummus with Red Lentils

93. Hummus with Light Cream Cheese

94. Hummus with Red Curry Paste and Coconut Milk

95. Stimulating Walnut Hummus

96. Hummus with Honey and Sriracha

97. Hummus with Maple Syrup and Vanilla Extract

98. Humus with Miso

Conclusion

Introduction

Hummus is a very popular creamy, thick spread or dip that is served in different restaurants all over the world. It is normally made from cooked, mashed chickpeas along with other healthy ingredients like olive oil, tahini, garlic and salt. The dip has long been served in North Africa and Middle Eastern countries. At present, it is also being served across Europe and North America.

According to statistics, hummus is the most widely consumed in the United States and Middle Eastern today. Around 15 million Americans in 2008 were reported eating humus regularly. These individuals are enjoying the many benefits of hummus.

For those who are new to hummus and have limited knowledge on preparing the dip, this book is for you. But before you start preparing your dip, you should know first how and where it started. Some people consider hummus as an ancient food that was eaten by honorable figures in the Middle East.

The very first hummus was made in the 13th century in Egypt, but the recipe used during that time were different from today since some people omitted tahini and replaced it with other nuts. At present, hummus still has an important role in the diet of many health conscious individuals not just in the Middle East but all over the world.

Hummus is known to be a healthy food because of its contents. Each ingredient added into it has health benefits. So, if you love dips but want to keep your body healthy and fit, start adding hummus in your everyday diet.

Health Benefits of Hummus

Hummus is a popular dip, paste or spread made of tahini and chickpeas that is normally consumed together with pita or any other flat bread most of the time during breakfast. Its texture and consistency is somewhat similar to peanut butter. As mentioned earlier, it is widely used in the Middle East particularly in countries like Turkey, Lebanon, Syria, Cyprus, and Israel. It is very popular not only because it tastes really good, but also it is very nutritious.

The primary ingredients for hummus are tahini and chickpeas. Chickpeas are commonly known as garbanzo beans, while tahini refers to the sesame paste. Be careful in using tahini because it has a strong flavor; therefore, only a small amount should be added. Some people would make variations by omitting tahini and replacing it with other nuts. Other ingredients of hummus are salt, paprika, lemon juice, olive oil and fresh garlic. This dish is very easy to prepare; simply process all the ingredients until they produce a smooth paste. Below are some of the health benefits of hummus found in each ingredient.

Chickpeas Health Benefits

Chickpeas are very nutritious because they do not contain any saturated fats or cholesterol. They contain a good amount of protein. This is the reason why vegetarians love hummus. Chickpeas are also very effective in preventing the cholesterol build up in the blood vessels. Aside from that, it can also help maintain the right level of blood sugar.

Tahini Health Benefits

Tahini contains a huge amount of calories and fats. But, since only a small amount of it is being added to hummus, there is no need for you to worry. Just like chickpeas, it is also rich in protein. It is also a good source of calcium.

Olive Oil Health Benefits

Olive oil is also very healthy. It contains healthy fat and is rich in monounsaturated fat, but is low in saturated fat. It helps regulate cholesterol and it helps keeps your heart protected against different diseases.

Garlic and Lemon Juice Health Benefits

Lemon juice and garlic, on the other hand, are rich in antioxidants that help lower oxidative stress in the body. They likewise work to boost immune functions and protect you against viruses and bacteria.

Hummus Total Health Benefits

As a whole, hummus contains lots of Omega 3 fatty acids, which are perfect for boosting intelligence and keeping your heart healthy. Also, this dip contains vitamin B6, amino acids, iron, copper, manganese and folic acid. The amino acids found in hummus are tyrosine, tryptophan and phenylalanine that can help you sleep well and uplift your mood.

Hummus is full of nutrients that can help you keep your lifestyle healthy. Include this in your everyday diet by using it as dressing to your pasta or salad, as a spread on your favorite sandwiches and wraps, as a side dish for the main courses, or as dip for pita or raw vegetables.

100 Easy to Prepare Hummus Recipes

Although there are lots of different brands of hummus available on the market today that use minimal ingredients, it is still best to make your own hummus free from preservatives. By making your own hummus, you are sure what is added in the recipe and you can get the complete health benefits of hummus. This dip is very simple to make; all you need are some basic ingredients and a blender or food processor.

1. Red Pepper Hummus

There are several variations to the classic hummus and this one includes roasted red peppers. This recipe will suit your taste buds. Just like any hummus recipe, preparing this dip is easy.

INGREDIENTS:

1 can drained and rinsed chickpeas
1 quartered garlic clove
1 tablespoon olive oil
1/2 red bell pepper
2 1/2 tablespoons fresh lemon juice
1/4 teaspoon freshly ground black pepper
1/4 teaspoon salt

INSTRUCTIONS:

•Pre-heat the broiler.
•Prepare the bell pepper by cutting it in half lengthwise, remove the seeds and membranes. On a foil-lined baking sheet, arrange the sliced bell pepper, skin side up.
•Flatten them using your hand. Broil until it turns black or for ten minutes. Cool and place in a Ziploc plastic bag- then seal. Allow it to stand for ten minutes. Remove the peel.
•In a food processor, place the bell pepper and the rest of the ingredients; process until it becomes smooth and slowly add olive oil until you achieve the desired consistency.

NUTRITIONAL VALUE:

Calories - 430
Total Fat - 10g
Cholesterol - 0
Total Carbohydrate - 67g
Dietary Fiber - 18g
Protein - 20g

2. Conventional Hummus

This hummus recipe can be a substitute for ranch seasoning that you can mix into ranch burgers, ranch dip or salad dressing. With this recipe, you don't have to buy salsa, which is full of preservatives. This hummus is healthy and delicious.

INGREDIENTS:

1 1/2 teaspoon salt
1/2 c. tahini
2 c. chickpeas
2 lemons for juicing
3 tablespoon olive oil
4 cloves garlic
7 c. water for the slow cooker

INSTRUCTIONS:

•Pour seven cups of water in your slow cooker and then add the dried chickpeas. Cover and cook for 6 hours on low or 4 hours on high overnight. Make sure that the chickpeas are soft enough. Remove the water and add the chickpeas in your blender or food processor.
•Add all the remaining ingredients in the food processor and process until smooth. Add a small amount of water if the mixture is too thick, and then process again until you achieve the needed consistency.

NUTRITIONAL VALUE:

Calories - 110
Total Fat - 5g
Cholesterol - 0%
Total Carbohydrate -13g
Dietary Fiber - 4g
Protein - 4g

3. Toasted Sesame Seeds Hummus

Instead of tahini, this recipe uses toasted sesame seeds. Just like any hummus recipe, this one is healthy and delicious. To make this dip even more interesting, use it in baked pita chips.

INGREDIENTS:

3 tablespoon sesame seeds
19 ounce garbanzo beans, drained (keep the juices)
¼ c. olive oil
1 tablespoon fresh lemon juice
1 teaspoon kosher salt
4-5 garlic cloves, whole

INSTRUCTIONS:

•Over medium heat, toast sesame seeds in a small skillet until golden; shake pan often.
•Make sure that the sesame seeds do not burn. Put aside.
•Place garlic cloves in the food processor and then pulse until minced. Add olive oil, kosher salt, beans and lemon juice to the processor and pulse until smooth.
•You can add 2 to 3 tbsp. of garbanzo juice, one tablespoon at a time if the mixture is too thick, until it achieves the needed consistency. Add toasted sesame seeds and then process again until smooth.
•Place in the fridge for one to two hours before using.

NUTRITIONAL VALUE:

Calories - 520
Total Fat - 20g
Cholesterol - 0%
Total Carbohydrate - 68g
Dietary Fiber - 19g
Protein - 22g

4. Rosemary Hummus

This hummus recipe has a Mediterranean twist. It is easy to prepare, cheap and very tasty. It is perfect as a spread or dip on chips, crackers, and bread, and is also best with grilled vegetables.

INGREDIENTS:

1 peeled clove garlic
1/4 c. balsamic vinegar
1/4 c. cold water
1/4 c. olive oil
2 (15.5 ounce) cans drained garbanzo beans
2 sprigs fresh rosemary
Salt and pepper to taste

INSTRUCTIONS:

•Remove rosemary leaves from its stem and then put the leaves in the food processor.
•Then add garlic and then pulse again until chopped finely. Add the garbanzo beans in the processor until well combined.
•Slowly add olive oil in portions in the food processor; scrape the sides of the bowl if needed. Add the balsamic vinegar and pulse until well blended.
•Taste and add more vinegar if needed, add one tablespoon at a time.
•Add water and pulse to produce a spreadable mixture. If needed, add more water, one tablespoon at a time.
•Add pepper and salt to taste.
•Refrigerate before serving.

NUTRITIONAL VALUE:

Calories - 157
Carbohydrates - 21 g
Cholesterol - 0 mg
Fat - 6.4 g
Fiber - 3.9 g
Protein - 4.4 g

5. Hummus with Paprika

There are thousands of variations of hummus that you can find online. People often add and tweak ingredients to satisfy their palate. This recipe is one of the well-loved versions of hummus. It still contains all the nutrition that you can find in the basic hummus.

INGREDIENTS:

⅓ cup tahini
1½ tsp. kosher salt
2 c. drained chickpeas, liquid reserved
2 minced garlic cloves
2 tablespoon reserved chickpea liquid, or water
2 tbsp. olive oil
3 ice cubes
6 dashes hot sauce
7 tbsp. freshly squeezed lemon juice
Paprika garnish

INSTRUCTIONS:

•Place all the ingredients except ice cubes, olive oil and paprika in a high-powered blender or food processor.
•Blend until the mixture becomes smooth, or for about 3 minutes.
•Add ice and then process until well mixed.
•Pour the mixture in the serving bowl and sprinkle paprika and olive oil on top.

NUTRITIONAL VALUE:

Calories - 70
Total Fat - 5 g
Cholesterol - 0 mg
Total Carbohydrate - 4 g
Dietary Fiber - 1 g
Protein - 2g

6. Tahini Free Hummus

This tahini- free hummus is perfect for your kid's sensitive taste buds. It is easy to prepare and only takes a few minutes.

INGREDIENTS:

1 (15 ounce) can drained garbanzo beans, liquid reserved
1 crushed clove garlic
1 tbsp. olive oil
1/2 tsp. salt
2 tsp. ground cumin

INSTRUCTIONS:

•In a food processor or blender, add garlic, olive oil, garbanzo beans, salt and cumin.
•Process the mixture on low speed, then slowly add the set- aside liquid until it achieves the needed consistency.

NUTRITIONAL VALUE:

Calories - 79.8
Total Fat - 2.4 g
Cholesterol - 0.0 mg
Total Carbohydrate - 12.4 g
Dietary Fiber - 2.4 g
Protein - 2.7 g

7. Nut Butter Hummus

If you love peanut butter, then this dip is for you. This hummus dip is perfect with veggies or tortilla chips. Just like any hummus, this one also contains all the nutrients found in basic hummus.

INGREDIENTS:

½ teaspoon Sea Salt
1½ tablespoon Nut Butter
2 c. cooked chickpeas
2 Cloves of Garlic
2 tablespoons Olive Oil
2 tablespoons Water
2+ tablespoons Lemon Juice

INSTRUCTIONS:

•Place all the ingredients in a high-powered blender or food processor and blend until smooth.
•To achieve the desired consistency and taste, add more water or lemon juice depending on what you want.

NUTRITIONAL VALUE:

Calories - 460
Total Fat - 15g
Cholesterol - 0%
Total Carbohydrate - 65g
Dietary Fiber - 18g
Protein - 20g

8. Avocado Flavored Hummus

This hummus recipe is just like any other hummus, where all you need to do is to add all the ingredients, including the avocados, in a high-powered blender or food processor and blend. The avocado makes the hummus creamier and taste really good.

INGREDIENTS:

1/4 c. lemon juice
1/4 c. tahini
2 (15 ounce) cans chickpeas, drained and rinsed
2 cloves minced garlic
2 medium peeled avocados, stone removed
Salt to taste

INSTRUCTIONS:

• Place all the ingredients in the food processor and blend until it becomes smooth.
• Add water as needed until you achieve the desired consistency.
• Transfer to a serving bowl and serve.

NUTRITIONAL VALUE:

Calories - 279
Fat - 17g
Cholesterol - 0
Total Carbohydrate - 23.4g
Fiber - 8.5g
Protein - 10g

9. Hummus with Parsley

This recipe is healthy, smooth and rich and is perfect with toasted pitas. Some people use this hummus recipe as a spread for sandwiches. Another way to enjoy this healthy dip is by spreading it on toasted rye with ripe tomatoes on top. You can also add hot peppers or red peppers.

INGREDIENTS:

1 pinch paprika
1 tbsp. olive oil or more if needed
1 tsp. minced fresh parsley
1 tsp. salt
1/3 c. tahini
1/4 c. lemon juice
2 c. garbanzo beans
2 minced garlic cloves

INSTRUCTIONS:

•Add tahini, garlic, garbanzo beans, salt and lemon juice in a food processor or blender.
•Pulse until it becomes smooth.
•Add olive oil in the garbanzo beans mixture through feed tube to make it even smoother.
•Pour the mixture in the serving bowl.
•Add more oil if needed.
•Sprinkle with parsley and paprika.

NUTRITIONAL VALUE:

Calories - 73.1
Total Fat - 3.6 g
Cholesterol - 0 mg
Total Carbohydrate - 8.5 g
Dietary Fiber - 1.8 g
Protein - 2.4 g

10. Oil-Free Hummus

This oil free hummus is as healthy and as delicious as the basic hummus. It is perfect as a dip for pretzel sticks. If you want it spicy you can add a few drops of hot sauce.

INGREDIENTS:

15 ounce can of chickpeas
Salt to taste
1/3 cup tahini
1/4 c. lemon juice
5-8 cloves garlic

INSTRUCTIONS:

•Add all the ingredients in a high-powered blender or food processor and blend until smooth.
•Transfer in an airtight container- it will last up to a week.

NUTRITIONAL VALUE:

- Calories - 40
- Total Fat - 1g
- Cholesterol -0%
- Carbohydrates - 6g
- Dietary Fiber -2g
- Protein - 2g

11. Cumin-Coriander Combo Hummus

For this recipe, you need to prepare first the coriander and cumin. Toast the mentioned ingredients in a sauté pan over low heat until lightly toasted and aromatic, for about two minutes. Allow it to cool down, grind using mortar and pestle or coffee grinder. Peel the chickpeas before adding them in the food processor, to produce a smoother hummus.

INGREDIENTS:

2 large minced garlic cloves
2 tbsp. extra-virgin olive oil, add more for garnish
3 tbsp. warm water, add more if needed
Finely chopped parsley, for garnish, optional
Kosher salt
Pinch of cayenne pepper
Toasted pine nuts, for garnish, optional
1 1/2 c. cooked garbanzo beans
1 1/2 tbsp. tahini
3 1/2 tbsp. freshly squeezed lemon juice, add more if needed
1/4 tsp. ground toasted cumin/coriander combo

INSTRUCTIONS:

•In your food processor bowl, place the garlic first, and then pulse for a few minutes to grind it. Add the lemon juice, tahini, garbanzo beans, spices, ¾ tsp salt, olive oil and water. Combine until smooth; scrape down the bowl as you continue blending.
•Taste- if needed, add salt or lemon juice, to achieve the right balance of flavors. The dip will taste bright with lemon juice, rather than heavy with tahini and beans. You can also add more water, little by little, to adjust the consistency.
•Before serving, drizzle with olive oil and sprinkle parsley and nuts.

NUTRITIONAL VALUE:

Calories	64
Total Fat	2.3g
Cholesterol	0mg
Total Carbohydrates	8.6g
Dietary Fiber	2.5g
Protein	2.9g

12. Hummus with Cayenne Pepper Topped with Kalamata Olives

This recipe enhances the flavor of hummus. The kalamata olives intensify the standard tahini and chickpea combination. The outcomes are surprising and bold, the perfect dish to shake up a spread.

INGREDIENTS:

1 -2 tbsp. dark sesame oil
½ c. extra virgin olive oil
½ tsp. cayenne pepper
¼ c. chopped cilantro or ¼ cup parsley
¼ tsp. ground cumin
3 (19 oz.) cans chickpeas
3 lemons, juice of
3 medium garlic cloves
Kalamata olives

INSTRUCTIONS:

•Combine garlic, a quarter of chickpeas, cumin and lemon juice in a food processor and blend until smooth.
•Add the rest of the chickpeas and process; add olive oil and sesame oil; add pepper and salt to taste. If you have a smaller food processor, you need to blend the ingredients in batches.
•Process until smooth and creamy, adding olive oil gradually until you achieve the desired consistency.
•Transfer into a serving bowl, sprinkle cilantro or parsley and cayenne, and kalamata olives on top.

NUTRITIONAL VALUE:

Calories	305.2
Total Fat	14 g
Cholesterol	0 mg
Total Carbohydrate	38.2 g
Dietary Fiber	7.2 g
Protein	8.1 g

13. Delicious Sriracha Hummus

Adding sriracha in hummus will make your dip really exciting and hot. If in case you don't have garlic or vinegar, sriracha is a good substitute since it has a nice vinegar and garlic taste. You can use this type of hummus as a spread in your sandwich wrap, in a veggie burger or as dip.

INGREDIENTS:

1 clove garlic small clove preferably
1 tablespoon sriracha sauce
1 tablespoon water
1 teaspoon red wine vinegar
1/2 teaspoon cumin
1/2 teaspoon salt
15 ounce peeled garbanzo beans
2 tablespoon fresh lemon juice, about a half of a lemon
2 tablespoons olive oil

INSTRUCTIONS:

•Drain the garbanzo beans and peel off the skin
•Place sriracha sauce, vinegar, oil, garlic, lemon juice, water, salt and cumin in the food processor or high-powered blender and process for about one minute.
•Taste- you can add more sriracha if you want. To achieve the creaminess that you prefer, you can blend it longer.
•Perfect with pita chips or other finger foods that will taste better if you dip into it!

NUTRITIONAL VALUE:

Calories	470
Total Fat	13g
Cholesterol	0mg
Total Carbohydrate	69g
Dietary Fiber	18g
Protein	21g

14. Grilled Zucchini Hummus

This hummus dip is similar to Baba Ganoush, but instead of using eggplant, this recipe uses zucchini. The zucchini is pureed together with the basic ingredients of hummus to produce a healthier and tastier dip. It can be served hot or cold as a dip for soft pita bread, or as a spread in a wrap with veggies or grilled meat.

INGREDIENTS:

1 ½ pound roasted or grilled zucchini
⅛ cup lemon juice- plus more to taste
¼ cup tahini
½ teaspoon kosher salt, more to taste
½ teaspoon cracked pepper
¼ cup or more fresh herbs
1 tablespoon olive oil- Garnish
2-3 Cloves garlic

INSTRUCTIONS:

•Prepare the zucchini by cutting it into ½ inch thick strips. Brush some olive oil and grill until charred and soft. Place in the foil and allow them to steam to make it even softer.
•In a food processor or high-powered blender place grilled zucchini together with the other ingredients except for the oil and blend until smooth.
•If you prefer to roast the zucchini it is best to add some smoked paprika. Transfer the hummus in a bowl, drizzle some olive oil and serve.

NUTRITIONAL VALUE:

Calories	300
Total Fat	21g
Cholesterol	0mg
Total Carbohydrate	21g
Dietary Fiber	6g
Protein	9g

15. Jalapeno-Cilantro Hummus

This hummus recipe is definitely one of the most popular dips. This utterly tasty hummus dip is perfect together with tortilla chips or pita chips. This jalapeno cilantro hummus is easy to prepare and nutritious.

INGREDIENTS:

1 (15 oz.) can garbanzo beans, drained
1 c. fresh cilantro, or to taste
1 jalapeno pepper, stemmed and diced - or to taste
1 pinch garlic powder, or to taste
1 tbsp. olive oil, or as needed
2 diced cloves garlic
Salt and ground black pepper to taste

INSTRUCTIONS:

•In a food processor or high-powered blender, add all the ingredients and process until well mixed and smooth.
•Transfer in a serving bowl and serve chilled or hot.
•Serve.

NUTRITIONAL VALUE:

Calories	40
Carbohydrates	5.7 g
Cholesterol	0mg
Fat	1.4 g
Fiber	1.2 g
Protein	1.3 g

16. Chickpeas Soaked in Baking Soda Hummus

Just like other hummus, you can consider this recipe a dip, a spread on sandwiches, as a side dish for chicken kabobs, or you can eat it alone. There are lots of people who really love the taste of hummus so much that they eat it like an ice cream!

INGREDIENTS:

2 c. chickpeas, soaked overnight
4 cloves minced garlic
1 c. Tahini Paste
3 tablespoons of Lemon Juice
3 tablespoons of Olive Oil, plus more for drizzling on the top
Olive oil
1/2 tablespoon baking soda
1/2 tablespoon salt, or to taste
1/2 c. of water

INSTRUCTIONS:

•Prepare the chickpeas by soaking in water overnight. The following day, drain and wash the beans.
•In a medium size pot, pour enough water to cover the beans and add the baking soda.
•Bring to a boil and cook until tender, or for about 45 mins.
•Remove any of the foam that might accumulate during the cooking process.
•While waiting for the chickpeas to cook, prepare the other ingredients. Chop the garlic and roll out the lemon to extract the juice from it.
•Place the remaining ingredients (except water and olive oil) in a food processor, including the cooled beans and start blending to puree the mixture. Add water along the way. Continue with the process until the needed consistency is achieved.
•Transfer the mixture in a serving dish, sprinkle some paprika if you want and then add the olive oil on top.

NUTRITIONAL VALUE:

Calories	780
Total Fat	49g
Cholesterol	0%
Total Carbohydrate	68g
Dietary Fiber	19g
Protein	27g

17. Extra Creamy Hummus

This recipe will make hummus extra creamy, extra delicious and extra nutritious. It is best served while it is still warm; however, eating four cups of this in one sitting is such a challenge. You can store the remaining hummus in a plastic container with olive oil on top, so it will maintain its smoothness. Store it in the fridge and it can last for about a week or two. This recipe uses chickpea flour instead of the garbanzo beans.

INGREDIENTS:

3 cloves minced garlic
1 lemon, juice only
Pinch of ground cumin
Pinch of salt and pepper
Dash of hot sauce
2 1/2 C. water
1/4 C. water or stock for blending
1/4 C. Tahini
1/4 C. olive oil
3/4 C. Chickpea flour

INSTRUCTIONS:

•Chickpea flour can take a lot of water, so in preparing this dip you need to melt the flour first.
•Simmer water in a pan, then add the flour. It may seem like a smaller amount than the water, but it will swell really fast. Whisk until it begins to thicken. You might notice some lumps; but don't worry. Continue to simmer in the pan, stirring frequently for about 8-10 mins. or until it becomes thick over low heat.
•Place all the ingredients and the chickpea paste in the food processor. In case you have a smaller processor you can divide the ingredients into two.
•Process and add water and oil until it becomes creamy and smooth.

NUTRITIONAL VALUE:

Calories	280
Total Fat	22g
Cholesterol	0%
Total Carbohydrate	16g
Dietary Fiber	3g
Protein	7g

18. Jalapeno-Cumin Combo Hummus

Preparing hummus with jalapeno will only take a few minutes, and it is much healthier since there is no oil added into it. You can decrease or increase the ingredients as needed, particularly the jalapenos. Serve as a dip for pita chips or fresh vegetable slices. If you want a smoother dip, you can add more of the reserved beans.

INGREDIENTS:

1 (15 ounce) can garbanzo beans, drained, liquid reserved
2 ounces sliced fresh jalapeno peppers
2 tablespoons lemon juice
3 cloves minced garlic
1/2 teaspoon ground cumin

INSTRUCTIONS:

• Add garbanzo beans, lemon juice, jalapeno, garlic, cumin and one tablespoon of the reserved garbanzo liquid to your food processor.
•Process until well mixed and smooth.

NUTRITIONAL VALUE:

Calories	23
Carbohydrates	4.5 g
Cholesterol	0 mg
Fat	0.2 g
Fiber	0.9 g
Protein	1 g

19. Hummus with Smoked Paprika

The smoked paprika adds flavor to already tasty and yummy hummus. Your kids will also love this dip- perfect for their chips and fresh veggie cuts. This recipe is fast and easy to prepare.

INGREDIENTS:

1 1/2 tsp. salt
1 tsp. smoked paprika
1/2 c. tahini
2 (15 oz.) cans garbanzo beans (reserve juice)
5 garlic cloves
6 oz. fresh lemon juice
extra virgin olive oil

INSTRUCTIONS:

•Place all the ingredients except smoked paprika and olive oil, in a food processor bowl.
•Process until it becomes smooth. In case the mixture is too thick, you can add lemon juice, little by little.
•Transfer the hummus in a serving bowl and sprinkle it with smoked paprika and drizzle some olive oil.

NUTRITIONAL VALUE:

Calories	590
Total Fat	22.6 g
Cholesterol	0 mg
Total Carbohydrate	81.8 g
Dietary Fiber	16.8 g
Protein	21.8 g

20. Low-Fat Yogurt Hummus

If you are looking for something unique to serve your guests, this hummus with yogurt is the perfect solution. Best tasting hummus and also very healthy.

INGREDIENTS:

1 (19 oz.) can chickpeas, drained and rinsed
1 tbsp. chopped fresh parsley
1 tbsp. lemon juice
1 tsp. olive oil
1/4 c. plain low-fat yogurt
1/4 tsp. paprika
1/4 tsp. salt
1/8 tsp. pepper
3 minced garlic cloves, more if you like

INSTRUCTIONS:

•Combine everything in a blender or food processor and process until smooth.
•If needed, add more liquid to achieve a nice consistency; you can also add more yogurt.
•Refrigerate and chill.
•Perfect as veggie dip or with pitas.

NUTRITIONAL VALUE

Calories	123.3
Total Fat	2 g
Cholesterol	0.6 mg
Total Carbohydrate	21.8 g
Dietary Fiber	4.1 g
Protein	5.1 g

21. Cannellini Beans Hummus

For vegetarians, hummus is a good substitute that is full of protein. This dip is very simple and easy to prepare. You only need around 4 to 5 ingredients- process them in a food processor and you are all done. You can add extra ingredients to the hummus that will make it taste even more flavorful. You can serve hummus as spread for crackers and sandwiches.

INGREDIENTS:

1 c. of cannellini beans (white beans)
1 c. of garbanzo beans (chickpeas)
1 tablespoon pimentos (optional)
1 tablespoon pine nuts (optional)
1/2 teaspoon of salt
1/4 c. of olive oil
1/4 c. of Tahini
1/4 c. of water
2 medium size cloves of garlic
2 teaspoons lemon juice
3 teaspoons cumin

INSTRUCTIONS:

•Add all ingredients in a food processor or blender and process until smooth and creamy.
•Transfer to a serving bowl. Create swirls in a circle using the back of a spoon.
•Garnish with pine nuts, pimentos and drizzle with olive oil. You can also sprinkle it with cumin.

NUTRITIONAL VALUE:

Calories	620
Total Fat	27g
Cholesterol	0%
Total Carbohydrate	76g
Dietary Fiber	26g
Sugars	8g
Protein	26g

22. Guacamole Hummus

You can serve this hummus dip for lunch with corn chips. However, there are some that serve it in the afternoon during snack time and also at dinner. You can have this also during a pool party and serve it in a giant bowl so everybody will enjoy this great tasting dip.

INGREDIENTS:

1 cup of medium salsa (Chunky mild)
1 pint hummus (any flavor)
151/2 oz. black beans (drained)
24 ounce guacamole

INSTRUCTIONS:

•Place everything in a bowl and mix by hand and refrigerate to chill.
•Serve as dip with corn chips, crackers and other fresh veggies.

NUTRITIONAL VALUE:

Calories	350
Total Fat	12g
Cholesterol	0%
Total Carbohydrate	47g
Dietary Fiber	19g
Protein	20g

23. Organic Arugula Hummus

This hummus recipe is a variation to the traditional hummus dip that is very nutritious, tasty and easy to make. It is rich in protein and can be served together with any kind of bread or veggies for dinner or lunch. The spicy flavor of Arugula gives additional hotness to this dip.

INGREDIENTS:

1 (16 ounce) Chickpeas / Garbanzo
1 cup Organic Baby Arugula
2 tablespoon Olive Oil
2 teaspoon lemon Juice
4 to 5 Garlic cloves
8 Peppercorns
Red pepper flakes and Dried Basil leaves – for garnish
Salt to taste

INSTRUCTIONS:

•Prepare chickpeas, remove the liquid and rinse.
•Place all the ingredients in a food processor or high-powered blender until it becomes smooth. You can add some water if the mixture is too thick.
•Transfer the mixture in a serving bowl and garnish it with basil leaves, red pepper flakes.
•Serve together with pita bread, veggies or any type of bread.

NUTRITIONAL VALUE:

Calories	500
Total Fat	15g
Cholesterol	0%
Total Carbohydrate	74g
Dietary Fiber	21g
Protein	23g

24. Protein Rich Tofu Hummus

This variation of hummus is protein rich and to add extra creaminess, peanut butter is used instead of tahini. The result is a creamy and delicious protein rich hummus.

INGREDIENTS:

2 tbsp. creamy peanut butter
2 tbsp. olive oil
3 cloves garlic
1 (19 oz.) can garbanzo beans, drained
1/2 c. diced silken tofu
1/4 c. lemon juice

INSTRUCTIONS:

•Place peanut butter, garlic, garbanzo beans, lemon juice, olive oil and tofu in a food processor or blender.
•Process until the mixture becomes smooth and creamy.
•Transfer in a serving bowl and chill until it is time to serve.

NUTRITIONAL VALUE:

Calories	296
Carbohydrates	40.5 g
Cholesterol	0 mg
Fat	9.5 g
Fiber	10.9 g
Protein	14.6 g

25. Simple Olive Hummus

This recipe is simple, cost less and satisfying and it only takes five minutes to prepare. It is perfect for late-night snack or during cocktails. Serve with pita wedges or fresh veggies. Leftovers can be stored in the fridge for up to 7 days.

INGREDIENTS:

1 (15 oz.) can garbanzo beans, drained
2 cloves minced garlic
3 tbsp. extra-virgin olive oil
2 tsp. chopped fresh basil
1 1/2 tsp. chopped fresh parsley
1/3 c. pimento-stuffed Manzanilla olives
1/4 c. lemon juice
1/4 tsp. salt
1/8 tsp. ground black pepper

INSTRUCTIONS:

•Combine garbanzo beans, garlic, olive oil, fresh basil, fresh parsley, lemon juice, salt, black pepper and manzanilla olives in a blender or food processor.
•Process until the mixture becomes smooth.

NUTRITIONAL VALUE:

Calories	130
Carbohydrates	11.9 g
Cholesterol	0 mg
Fat	8.3 g
Fiber	2.2 g
Protein	2.5 g

26. Cashew Nuts Hummus

As compared to other hummus recipes, this one is light and creamy, perfect for those who love to eat raw veggies. You can use this recipe as a veggie dip or a condiment to stir-fried veggies and rice.

INGREDIENTS:

1 c. soaked raw cashews
1 tbsp. raw organic tahini
1 tsp. organic minced garlic
1/4 tsp. organic onion powder
2 tbsp. extra virgin olive oil
Juice from 1 fresh lemon
Pinch of sea salt, to taste

INSTRUCTIONS:

•Place the raw tahini, extra virgin olive oil, garlic powder, lemon juice, sea salt, onion powder and soaked cashews in a food processor and pulse until smooth and creamy.
•If you want it to become creamier, add extra virgin olive oil.
•If you prefer a stronger tahini taste, you can add 1 tbsp. of tahini. Adjust the seasonings depending on your taste.
•If one lemon does not produce enough juice, you can use two lemons.
•Transfer in a covered glass bowl and refrigerate. The flavors become better and become thicker as it chills.
•Perfect as dip for fresh vegetables such as zucchini sticks, broccoli, carrot sticks, red pepper strips, cucumber sticks and yellow squash sticks.

NUTRITIONAL VALUE:

Calories	400
Total Fat	34g
Cholesterol	0mg
Total Carbohydrate	21g
Dietary Fiber	3g
Protein	11g

27. Element Rich Hummus

Himalayan salt is not just an ordinary salt- it contains 84 elements that are already found in the body. It helps regulate the water content of your body, promotes blood sugar health and reduces the signs of aging. It also regulates your sleep, promotes bone strength and many other health benefits. Therefore, this recipe is much healthier as compared to other hummus recipe.

INGREDIENTS:

1 ½ c. (250g) cooked chickpeas
½ small lemon, juiced
¼ c. (60ml) hulled tahini
2 cloves roughly chopped garlic
2 tbsp. olive oil
4 c. water
 Pink Himalayan salt

INSTRUCTIONS:

First, add the chickpeas in your food processor. Process the chickpeas until it becomes a clumpy and coarse powder, then add the Himalayan salt, lemon juice, tahini, garlic and olive oil before blending again.
Add one tablespoon of water at a time until the mixture becomes smooth. Taste, add more salt, tahini or lemon if needed until it satisfy your taste buds.
Transfer the mixture in an airtight container and refrigerate until it is time for you to serve it.

NUTRITIONAL VALUE:

Calories 420
Total Fat 18g
Cholesterol   0%
Total Carbohydrate 52g
Dietary Fiber 15g
Protein 17g

28. Creamy Cookie Dough Hummus

This recipe is very different from the usual hummus because it has a sweet, delicious taste. This hummus is perfect as dip for your fresh veggies or as a spread on a wrap with chopped apples or granola.

INGREDIENTS:

1 (15 oz.) can garbanzo beans, drained
1 1/2 tbsp. peanut butter
1 c. hot water
1 pinch ground cinnamon
1 tbsp. ground flax seed
1 tbsp. instant oatmeal
1 tbsp. raisins
1 tbsp. shredded coconut
1 tsp. ground cinnamon
1 tsp. maple syrup
1 tsp. vanilla extract
1/2 tsp. canola oil
1/4 c. unsweetened applesauce

INSTRUCTIONS:

•Place cinnamon and raisins in a bowl and add hot water. Let it stand for ten minutes, then drain.
•Place peanut butter, canola oil, ground flaxseed, applesauce, maple syrup, and vanilla extract in a food processor and then blend until smooth. With the blade still spinning, add the garbanzo beans, instant oatmeal, coconut and drained raisins and cinnamon slowly.
•Process until the mixture becomes smooth and creamy.

NUTRITIONAL VALUE:

Calories	33
Carbohydrates	4.9 g
Cholesterol	0 mg
Fat	1.1 g
Fiber	1 g
Protein	1.1 g

29. Italian Style Hummus

If you are thinking what to prepare for your family's snack or if you want a light lunch, spread this hummus on your toasted French bread. You can also serve this cold or warm with pita, as an appetizer.

INGREDIENTS:

1 (15.5 oz.) can cannellini beans, drained
1 bunch chopped fresh basil
1 c. non-fat cottage cheese
1 clove minced garlic
1 pint coarsely chopped grape tomatoes
Salt and pepper to taste

INSTRUCTIONS:

•In a food processor or blender, combine beans, garlic, tomatoes, cottage cheese, basil, salt and pepper until smooth.
•Place in a serving bowl and serve hot or cold.

NUTRITIONAL VALUE:

Calories	59
Carbohydrates	9.3 g
Cholesterol	1 mg
Fat	0.3 g
Fiber	2.1 g
Protein	5.2 g

30. Two Beans Hummus

This is a great recipe using two types of beans – soy beans and dried garbanzo beans. You can cook the beans first in a pressure cooker. It is best to soak the beans overnight and then simmer it for 2 hours in the morning.

INGREDIENTS:

1 bay leaf
1 quartered onion
1 c. vegetable broth
3 c. water
2 cloves crushed garlic
1 lemon, juiced
2 tbsp. soy sauce
Black pepper to taste
1/4 c. dried soybeans
1/4 c. tahini
1/4 c. chopped fresh parsley
3/4 c. dry garbanzo beans

INSTRUCTIONS:

•Cook the soybeans and garbanzos first in a pressure cooker together with onion and bay leaf. Pour the vegetable broth and enough water to cover the beans by one inch.
•Cover and set the pressure at high. Let the pressure drop naturally. Drain and reserve the liquid.
•Transfer the beans in the food processor. Add lemon juice, tahini, garlic, black pepper and soy sauce; process until it becomes smooth. If you want a thinner hummus, you can add some cooking liquid.
•Transfer the mixture in a serving bowl, and add in the parsley.

NUTRITIONAL VALUE:

Calories	161
Carbohydrates	20.2 g
Cholesterol	0 mg
Fat	6.4 g
Fiber	5.9 g
Protein	8 g

31. Fiesta Style Hummus

This fiesta style hummus is very yummy and it tastes like guacamole, but it is more flavorful. It is easy to prepare. All you have to do is to combine all the ingredients in a blender or food processor and process. You don't have to follow the exact measurement for the ingredients- you can add more depending on your preference.

INGREDIENTS:

1 tbsp. olive oil as needed
1 tsp. kosher salt
1 peeled and pitted avocado
1/2 c. fresh cilantro leaves
2 cloves minced garlic
1/3 c. orange juice
1/3 c. tahini
2 (15.5 oz.) cans drained garbanzo beans, liquid reserved
3 fresh jalapeno chiles- deseeded

INSTRUCTIONS:

•Place the garlic, jalapeno, cilantro, garbanzo beans, orange juice, avocado, salt and tahini in the bowl of a blender or food processor.
•Process until the mixture becomes smooth.
•Add reserve liquid from garbanzo beans or olive oil to adjust the thickness. Keep it in the fridge for one hour before serving.

NUTRITIONAL VALUE:

Calories	69
Carbohydrates	8.1 g
Cholesterol	0 mg
Fat	3.5 g
Fiber	2.1 g
Protein	2.2 g

32. Zesty Hummus-Like Spread

This zesty hummus is a delicious variation of the traditional hummus. The Italian and creamy salad dressing makes this recipe extra yummy. You can garnish it with spinach or red pepper. It is delicious served with pita bread or bagels.

INGREDIENTS:

1 (15 oz.) can garbanzo beans
1 red bell pepper, seeded and chopped
1 tsp. dried oregano
1/2 c. creamy salad dressing
1/2 tsp. garlic powder
1/2 tsp. sesame seeds
1/4 c. Italian-style salad dressing

INSTRUCTIONS:

•Place garbanzo beans, creamy salad dressing, sesame seeds, Italian-style salad dressing, oregano, garlic powder, and ½ red bell pepper in a blender or food processor.
•Pulse until smooth and creamy.
•Spread on a pita or bagel, garnish with spinach as well as the leftover bell pepper, or serve as a dip for your crackers- add some bell pepper cubes as garnish.

NUTRITIONAL VALUE:

Calories	57
Carbohydrates	5.9 g
Cholesterol	2 mg
Fat	3.3 g
Fiber	1 g
Protein	1 g

33. Spicy Five Pepper Hummus

If you want something spicy, this five pepper hummus is what you need. As the name implies, this hummus recipe contains 5 different peppers that will complement your pita chips or your baked whole wheat crackers. If you prefer less heat, you can remove the pepper seeds.

INGREDIENTS:

1 (15.5 oz.) can drained garbanzo beans, liquid reserved
1 tbsp. ground cumin
1 tbsp. olive oil
1 tbsp. sesame seeds
1 Cubanelle pepper
1 seeded and chopped red bell pepper
1/3 c. red pepper flakes, or to taste
2 tbsp. cayenne pepper
2 chopped jalapeno peppers
2 chopped serrano peppers
4 cloves minced garlic
5 tbsp. chopped canned banana peppers

INSTRUCTIONS:

• Place half of the garbanzo beans with half of the banana, Serrano, bell and cubanelle peppers in a food processor or blender.
• Also add red pepper flakes to taste, cayenne pepper, olive oil, cumin and sesame seeds in the blender or food processor. Blend until well combined.
• Add in the rest of the peppers and garbanzo beans.
• Add in one tablespoon of reserved garbanzo liquid, or the amount needed to thin the mixture into the desired smoothness, and pulse until smooth.

NUTRITIONAL VALUE:

Calories	21 kcal
Carbohydrates	3.3 g
Cholesterol	0 mg
Fat	0.7 g
Fiber	0.9 g
Protein	0.7 g

34. Sweet Potatoes Hummus

This is one of the most flavorful hummus recipes because of the sweetness and yumminess that the sweet potatoes provide. It is also a very healthy dip or spread. It is gluten-free, low in calories and vegan recipe. Who wouldn't love this healthy, flavorful and versatile recipe? You can dip pita chips and fresh veggies in it for an afternoon snack. Also, it can be used as a spread on a wrap for a healthy lunch.

INGREDIENTS:

¼ c. fresh lemon juice
¼ c. tahini
1 can (15 oz.) drained chickpeas, rinsed
1 clove garlic, halved
1 large sweet potato
1 teaspoon ground coriander
1 teaspoon ground cumin
1 teaspoon sea salt
2 teaspoon smoked paprika
3 tablespoons extra virgin olive oil

INSTRUCTIONS:

•Peel and cut sweet potato into 1 ½ inch cubes. Place sweet potato cubes on a pan with water and boil over medium high heat. As soon as it starts to boil, reduce the heat to low and simmer for fifteen to twenty minutes, or until the sweet potatoes are soft and tender. Let the potatoes cool down.
•In a large food processor, place cooked sweet potatoes together with the other ingredients. Cover and blend until smooth.
•If needed, add one tablespoon of water, one at a time until you achieve the desired consistency.
•Cover and chill for two hours to allow the flavors to blend.

NUTRITIONAL VALUE:

Calories	47
Fat	3g
Carbohydrates	3 g
Fiber	1 g
Protein	1 g
Cholesterol	0 mg

35. Sage and Oregano Hummus

This easy to prepare and delicious hummus variation is one of the favorite dips for your chips and spread for any type of bread.

INGREDIENTS:

1 1/2 tsp. dried basil
1 1/2 tsp. dried oregano
1 1/2 tsp. dried parsley
1 1/2 tsp. dried sage
1 tbsp. lemon juice
1 tbsp. olive oil
1/4 c. chopped red onion
2 (15 oz.) cans garbanzo beans, drained
3 tbsp. chopped roasted garlic

INSTRUCTIONS:

•Combine onions and garlic in a blender or food processor until finely chopped. Pour the garbanzo beans, one can at a time, and then blend again to puree.
•Add in basil, lemon juice, sage, olive oil, oregano, and parsley; blend until the mixture becomes smooth and creamy.

NUTRITIONAL VALUE:

Calories	108 kcal
Carbohydrates	17.9 g
Cholesterol	0 mg
Fat	2.6 g
Fiber	3.5 g
Protein	3.8 g

36. Black Beans-Jalapeno Humus

If you aim to get more fiber in your diet, this recipe will provide more fiber than the traditional hummus recipe. A half cup of black beans contains 7g of protein and 6g of fiber. Although chickpeas contain the same amount of protein and 5g of fibers, black beans has higher amount of iron, vitamin B1, magnesium and potassium.

INGREDIENTS:

1 peeled clove garlic
1 small chopped jalapeño pepper
1 tbsp. tahini
2 tbsp. olive oil
1 can(14 oz.) black beans, drained and rinsed
Juice from one lemon
Salt and pepper to taste

INSTRUCTIONS:

•Add the jalapeno pepper and garlic to a blender or food processor and blend. Add the rest of the ingredients and blend until smooth.
•You can use it right away or store in an airtight glass container and refrigerate- this will last up to a week.

NUTRITIONAL VALUE:

Calories	190
Total Fat	9g
Cholesterol	0%
Total Carbohydrate	24g
Dietary Fiber	10g
Protein	8g

37. Pine Nuts and Sweet Basil Hummus

Pine nuts will add creaminess in your hummus. You will surely love the taste when pine nuts, basil, Tabasco and the basic ingredients of hummus are combined. Serve best together with pita wedges, rustic bread or crackers.

INGREDIENTS:

1 1/2 to 2 tsp. salt
1 tsp. tomato paste
1/3 c. fresh lemon juice
1/4 c. olive oil
1/4 c. pine nuts
2 15-oz. cans drained garbanzo beans
2 c. sweet basil leaves, packed
3 cloves minced garlic
Several dashes Tabasco
Up to 1/4 c. water

INSTRUCTIONS:

•In a small skillet, heat the pine nuts over medium high heat. Stir once they start to brown. Transfer into a bowl when most of the nuts have turned light browned until cool. Keep some pine nuts aside for garnishing.
•Place garlic and basil leaves in the food processor. Process until chopped finely. Add the garbanzo beans, pine nuts, salt, Tabasco, olive oil, tomato paste and lemon juice.
•Pulse until the mixture is smooth. Add more salt, lemon juice or Tabasco to taste. Add water if needed to achieve the desired consistency.
•Transfer in a serving bowl and drizzle some olive oil on top of it. Sprinkle some toasted pine nuts on top. Serve together with crackers, bread or pita wedges.

NUTRITIONAL VALUE:

Calories	1280
Total Fat	43g
Cholesterol	0%
Total Carbohydrate	179g
Dietary Fiber	49g
Protein	56g

38. Cauliflower Hummus

This light cauliflower dip is the same with the traditional hummus, the only difference is that instead of chickpeas this recipe uses cauliflower. This is a creamy, nutritious dip to enjoy with some bread, crackers or fresh veggies.

INGREDIENTS:

1 pound cauliflower florets
1 tbsp. lemon juice
1 tsp. coriander seeds
1 tsp. cumin seeds
1/4 c. tahini
1-2 cloves of garlic
2 tbsp. olive oil
Salt
2 tbsp. finely chopped parsley or cilantro

INSTRUCTIONS:

•Steam the cauliflower for 15 mins. or until very soft. Alternative way to soften florets is to place the cauliflower florets in a saucepan with water and boil. Reduce the heat to low, and simmer for 10 mins. or until it is very soft. Make sure that the cauliflower is not water logged before you continue with the process.
•As you wait for the cauliflower, you can work on the spices. In a small skillet, toast cumin and coriander over medium-low heat for five minutes or until they turn lightly brown- shake often. Let the spices cool down, then powder them using a mortar and pestle or a food processor.
•Place the powdered spices, steamed and cooled cauliflower and the rest of the ingredients, except for parsley or cilantro, in a food processor, and pulse until the mixture is smooth and creamy.
•If the dip is too thick, add water, one tablespoon at a time, until it achieves the desired consistency.
•For a creamier hummus you can add more tahini.
•Garnish with chopped parsley or cilantro.

NUTRITIONAL VALUE:

Calories	130
Total Fat	10g
Cholesterol	0%
Total Carbohydrate	8g
Dietary Fiber	3g
Protein	4g

39. Wasabi Hummus

Have you tasted this unique hummus with a sushi-like variation? For those who prefer a really hot dip, this recipe is for you. Wasabi is known for its hot and strong taste, while hummus is popular because it is delicious and at the same time nutritious.

INGREDIENTS:

1 (15 oz.) can chickpeas, drained (reserve liquid)
1 clove garlic
1 tbsp. tahini (optional)
1 tbsp. wasabi powder
1/4 tsp. ground black pepper
2 tbsp. lemon juice
2 tbsp. olive oil, or more to taste
3 tbsp. soy sauce

INSTRUCTIONS:

•Place ½ of the chickpeas, olive oil, garlic, soy sauce, tahini, black pepper, lemon juice and wasabi powder in a blender or food processor.
•Process until the mixture becomes smooth and creamy. Scrape the sides of the blender or food processor bowl with a spatula to make sure that ingredients are well mixed. Pour the hummus into a serving bowl.
•Place the remaining chickpeas in the blender, keep five to seven beans for later use.
•Process until smooth. Add the reserve liquid if needed until it achieves the needed consistency. Add the second mixture to the first mixture and stir.
•Using the back of the spoon, create a shallow pool in the middle of the dip. Garnish with reserved chickpeas and olive oil.
•Use plastic wrap to cover the bowl and refrigerate for one hour.

NUTRITIONAL VALUE:

Calories	119 kcal
Carbohydrates	12.9 g
Cholesterol	0 mg
Fat	6.4 g
Fiber	2.7 g
Protein	3.4 g

40. Cucumber with Greek Yogurt Hummus

Remove the chickpeas skin to have the smoothest, silkiest hummus. Cucumber will add color and taste in your traditional hummus. Peel the cucumber, remove the seeds and chop. This will make your hummus very healthy and delicious.

INGREDIENTS:

⅓ c. finely diced parsely
½ c. of cucumber
1 teaspoon olive oil
2 c. of chick peas
2 cloves minced garlic
2 tablespoons plain Greek yogurt
9 tablespoons of tahini
Juice of half a lemon
Up to ⅓ cup of water

INSTRUCTIONS:

•Add tahini, lemon juice, tahini, olive oil, garlic, parsley, cucumber and yogurt in the bowl of a blender or food processor and process until smooth. If the mixture is too thick, add water, little by little.
•Add the chickpeas slowly to make sure that you incorporated it fully. Use plastic spatula to scrape down the sides and stir.
•Once all the chickpeas are added, you can add more water if needed and black pepper and salt to taste.
•Transfer in a serving bowl, put toasted pine nuts on top and drizzle with olive oil.

NUTRITIONAL VALUE:

Calories	230
Total Fat	9g
Cholesterol	0%
Total Carbohydrate	29g
Dietary Fiber	8g
Protein	10g

41. Roasted Carrot Hummus

Are you thinking of something new and nutritious to prepare for lunch time or snack? This roasted carrot hummus is a good variation for the traditional hummus, perfect with pita bread or fresh, raw veggies.

INGREDIENTS:

For the Roasted Carrots:
1 tsp. extra virgin olive oil
6 oz. carrots, chopped (1/2 inch thick round)
Salt and pepper

For the Hummus:
¼ c. extra virgin olive oil
¼ c. water
¼ tsp. paprika
¼ tsp. salt
1 clove garlic
16 oz. can drained chickpeas
2 tbsp. tahini
2 tsp. lemon juice
Pinch of cayenne pepper

INSTRUCTIONS:

How to Roast the Carrots:
•Pre-heat your oven to 425° Fahrenheit.
•Put the carrots in the baking dish and drizzle the olive oil on top of it. Sprinkle some pepper and salt and use spoon to toss. Place the carrots in the pre-heated oven and roast until it becomes soft. After 15 mins. of roasting, stir and then continue roasting for a total of 25 mins. Put aside and allow it to cool down slightly.

Preparing the Hummus:
•Add the roasted carrots and the other ingredients in a food processor or blender. Blend for two minutes or until smooth. If the mixture is too thick add more water or olive oil, one tablespoon at a time. Once you achieve the desired consistency transfer in a serving bowl and serve.

NUTRITIONAL VALUE:

Calories	73
Total Fat	2.0g
Total Carbohydrates	12.0g
Dietary Fiber	2.4g
Protein	2.6g

42. Black-Eyed Peas-Garlic Hummus

This recipe is smokey, flavorful and healthy that goes well with crackers, fresh raw vegetables or crispy bread. Instead of using canned black eyed peas, use the dried ones since it tastes much better.

INGREDIENTS:

¼ c. tahini
¼ tsp. dried crushed red pepper
½ c. extra-virgin olive oil, divided
½ c. fresh lemon juice
½ tsp. freshly ground black pepper
½ tsp. onion powder
1 ½ c. dried black-eyed peas
1 garlic bulb
1 tsp. table salt
2 tbsp. olive oil

INSTRUCTIONS:

• In a bowl of water, soak black eyed peas for twenty minutes. Drain.
• In a Dutch oven, place the black eyed peas with three cups of water. Boil. Cover and
• lower the heat- let it boil until the peas are very soft or for 35 mins.
• Soak black-eyed peas in a bowl with enough water to cover for 20 minutes. Drain and set aside.
• While waiting for the black-eyed peas to cook, pre-heat your oven to 400 degrees
• Fahrenheit. Remove the pointed end of the garlic and place them on aluminum foil. Drizzle olive oil and then fold to seal. Place in the oven and cook for forty minutes. Allow it to cool down.
• Place garlic in a food processor to squeeze pulp. Add lemon juice, peas, and the rest of the ingredients. Process until smooth or for about two minutes.
• Serve together with pretzel chips, pita chips or wedges of fresh veggies.

NUTRITIONAL VALUE:

Calories	550
Total Fat	47g
Cholesterol	0%
Total Carbohydrate	26g
Dietary Fiber	2g
Protein	11g

43. Rosemary Pumpkin and Roasted Garlic Hummus

If you haven't tried this recipe yet, maybe this is the right time to do so. The combination of rosemary, pumpkin and roasted garlic is heaven. As compared to other hummus recipe, this one is more creamy and really tastes good.

INGREDIENTS:

½ tsp. finely minced fresh rosemary (more to taste)
⅔ cup pumpkin puree
1 can chickpeas, drained and rinsed
1 tbsp. maple syrup or honey
1-2 cloves roasted garlic
2 tbsp. olive oil
2 tbsp. water
Salt to taste

INSTRUCTIONS:

•Roast the garlic first, peel the garlic and simmer in a saucepan with olive oil for about fifteen to twenty minutes at low-medium heat. By doing this, the garlic will have a roasted flavor and at the same you will get garlic infused olive oil.
•Place all the ingredients in a food processor or blender, except for rosemary, and process until smooth. Add more water or oil if the mixture is too thick. Add in the rosemary at the end.
•Transfer in a serving bowl with warm naan, carrots, roasted veggies, apple slices, crackers or wheat toast.

NUTRITIONAL VALUE:

Calories	111
Total fat	5g
Cholesterol	0
Total Carbohydrates	14g
Protein	4g

44. Cilantro-Lime Combo Hummus

This cilantro-lime combo hummus with crushed red peppers provides sweet and spicy taste that you will really love. This dip is combined with the basic hummus ingredients with garnishes on top so you can control how much flavor you would like in every bite.

INGREDIENTS:

¼ c. Chili & Cilantro Dip + additional for topping
¼ c. olive oil
¼ c. water
½ c. tahini
1 clove garlic
1 tsp. cumin
1 tsp. salt
2 15-oz cans chickpeas, drained and rinsed
2 lemons, juice and zest
2 tbsp. chopped cilantro

INSTRUCTIONS:

•Place tahini and zest and juice of lemons in a blender and pulse for one minute so that the mixture is smooth and creamy.
•Add garlic, salt, olive oil and cumin to blender and then blend again for another minute until well mixed.
•Then add half of the chickpeas to the blender and then blend for another minute. Add the rest of the chickpeas, water and the chili and cilantro dip and then blend again for another minute until it becomes smooth and creamy.
•Transfer the mixture in the serving dish and garnish with chopped cilantro and more chili and cilantro dip.
•Serve together with your favorite chips or veggies.

NUTRITIONAL VALUE:

Calories	29
Total Fat	0.8g
Total Carbohydrates	4.5g
Dietary Fiber	0.1g
Protein	1.2g

45. Pepperoncini Hummus

This is a perfect dip during a party or you can spread on some bread for a quick lunch. It is more flavorful as compared to the basic hummus. You can use either hot or mild smoked paprika. You can also use green or black olives or both. Instead of using fresh garlic, you can use garlic powder.

INGREDIENTS:

1 (15 1/2 oz.) can chickpeas, drained & rinsed
1 ½ tsp. cumin
1 -2 oz. water (or liquid from chickpeas)
1 -2 tsp. pepperoncini brine
1 pepperoncini pepper, seeded & chopped
1 tbsp. fresh lemon juice
1 tbsp. fresh parsley, chopped
½ tsp. pepper
½ tsp. smoked paprika
¼ c. chopped olive
¼ tsp. garlic powder
⅛-½ tsp. salt
2 tbsp. tahini
3 tbsp. extra virgin olive oil

INSTRUCTIONS:

•Combine all the ingredients in the food processor bowl except for water and salt and blend until the mixture becomes smooth.
•With the food processor still running, add the hot water, teaspoon by teaspoon, until it achieves the desired consistency.
•The pepperoncini brine will make the humus a bit salty. If you prefer a salty dip, you can add more salt until you get the taste that you want.
•Transfer in the serving bowl. Make a hollow in the center of the hummus. Pour one tablespoon of olive oil and then dash some smoke paprika and parsley.

NUTRITIONAL VALUE:

Calories	754.1
Total Fat	43 g
Cholesterol	0 mg
Total Carbohydrate	78.6 g
Dietary Fiber	17 g
Protein	19.4 g

46. Healthy Curried Hummus

Garbanzo beans have a low glycemic index that helps keep the blood sugar steady and are very helpful for diabetics. The curry powder contains an antioxidant known as curcumin, which has anti-cancer and anti-inflammatory properties.

INGREDIENTS:

½ cup water
2 (15.5 oz.) cans garbanzo beans, rinsed and drained
2 tbsp. olive oil
3 garlic cloves crushed
4 tsp. curry powder
6 tbsp. fresh lemon juice
Hot sauce to taste
Salt to taste

INSTRUCTIONS:

•Place all the ingredients in a blender or food processor and process until smooth.
•Transfer the mixture into serving bowl and drizzle with olive oil.
•Serve together with pita chips.

NUTRITIONAL VALUE:

Calories	84
Total Fat	2.4g
Cholesterol	0mg
Total Carbohydrates	13.4g
Dietary Fiber	2.6g
Protein	2.8g

47. Hummus with Pumpkin

This recipe is a healthy way of having hummus as your dip or spread. You can prepare more and store them in the fridge.

INGREDIENTS:

1 (15 oz.) can pumpkin (not pie mix)
1 garlic clove, chopped
1 tsp. ground cumin
1 tsp. olive oil
1/8 tsp. ground red pepper
2 tbsp. chopped fresh parsley
2 tbsp. fresh lemon juice
2 tbsp. tahini (sesame seed paste)
3/4 tsp. salt
4 pita breads, each cut into 8 wedges (6 inch)
Cooking spray

INSTRUCTIONS:

•Pre-heat your oven to 425°F. Prepare the baking sheets by spraying it with cooking spray. Arrange the pita wedges on it. Bake at 425 degrees Fahrenheit until toasted or for about six minutes.
•Add tahini, salt, cumin, olive oil, lemon juice, ground red pepper and garlic clove in a food processor or blender and blend until smooth. Add parsley until well combined.
•Transfer hummus in a serving bowl, sprinkle with toasted pumpkin seed kernels.
•Serve together with pita wedges.

NUTRITIONAL VALUE:

Calories	100.4
Total Fat	2.3 g
Cholesterol	0 mg
Total Carbohydrate	17.4 g
Dietary Fiber	1.1 g
Protein	3.2 g

48. Five Spices Orange Hummus

If you are a health conscious individual and you love the taste of orange combined with spices or peppers, this dish is for you. This dip is perfect with fresh raw veggies and pita wedges.

INGREDIENTS:

1 (15 ounce) can chickpeas, drained
1 garlic clove
1 tsp. Dijon mustard
1 tsp. low sodium soy sauce
¼ c. fresh parsley leaves
¼ c. orange juice
¼ tsp. ground coriander
¼ tsp. ground cumin
¼ tsp. ground ginger
¼ tsp. ground turmeric
¼ tsp. paprika
¼ tsp. salt
2 tbsp. chopped onions
2 tbsp. rice vinegar
2 tbsp. tahini (sesame seed paste)

INSTRUCTIONS:

•Place the garlic, onion and parsley in the food processor via food chute, and blend until minced.
•Add the orange juice and the rest of the ingredients, and pulse again until smooth.
•Transfer the hummus in a serving bowl together with crudité or pita triangle.

NUTRITIONAL VALUE:

Calories	92.2
Total Fat	2.5 g
Cholesterol	0 mg
Total Carbohydrate	14.6 g
Dietary Fiber	2.9 g
Protein	3.6 g

49. Spinach Hummus

The nutrients that the spinach provides will make this hummus a very healthy dip. It does not matter whether you use it as a dip or smoothie- it is a healthy addition. For those who love to eat green dishes, this recipe is for you. It tastes the same as the basic hummus, but it is more fun.

INGREDIENTS:

1 (15-oz.) can garbanzo beans drained- keep some liquid
1/2 tsp. cumin (optional)
1/2 tsp. salt, plus more to taste
1/3 c. tahini
2 c. baby spinach leaves
2 medium minced garlic cloves
3 tbsp. freshly squeezed lemon juice
Olive oil and paprika for topping, if desired.

INSTRUCTIONS:

•Place everything in the bowl of a food processor or in a blender, except for the reserved chickpeas liquid, and blend.
•Add the bean liquid if the mixture is too thick; pulse as you add the liquid, little by little, until it achieves the desired consistency.
•Taste and add more salt if needed.
•Transfer into the serving bowl and drizzle some olive oil and paprika on it.

NUTRITIONAL VALUE:

Calories	686.4
Total Fat	29.5 g
Cholesterol	0 mg
Total Carbohydrate	86.3 g
Dietary Fiber	20.6 g
Protein	27.6 g

50. Edamame Hummus

This is yet another variation of a healthy dip hummus. This time edamame is added. Many Lebanese prefer this type of hummus because of their religious belief about hummus and tabbouleh. It has an attractive green color because of edamame and spinach.

INGREDIENTS:

¾ c. boiled edamame, shells removed
1 c. frozen chopped spinach
1 (12 oz.) can chickpeas, drained
6 garlic cloves
½ c. tahini
¼-½ c. olive oil
1 tbsp. red pepper flakes

INSTRUCTIONS:

•Place everything in the bowl of the food processor.
•In case the mixture is too thick, you can add more olive oil, chickpeas liquid or water until it achieves the desired consistency.
•For leftovers, you can store it in the fridge.

NUTRITIONAL VALUE:

Calories	641.2
Total Fat	43.3 g
Cholesterol	0 mg
Total Carbohydrate	47.4 g
Dietary Fiber	13.1 g
Protein	23.5 g

51. Almond Hummus

This recipe uses almonds as a base that works well with tahini, lemon, olive oil and garlic. It is a highly recommended dip since both tahini and almonds come from sesame seeds, which contain a large amount of Omega-6 fatty acids. Tahini is a good source of amino acids, particularly methionine- it is high in vitamin E and gives fantastic flavor to just about any dish.

INGREDIENTS:

½ tbsp. grated lemon zest
⅓ c. water
¼ c. lemon juice
¼ tbsp. red pepper flakes
24 oz. cooked chickpeas
¾ c. roasted almond butter
¾ oz. garlic, chopped (10-12 small garlic cloves)
¾ tbsp. salt
Salt and pepper

INSTRUCTIONS:

•Place all the ingredients in a food processor except for water,until it becomes smooth
•Add water slowly, little by little, process as you add the water until the mixture becomes well blended and achieve the consistency needed.
•Transfer to an air tight container and refrigerate.

NUTRITIONAL VALUE:

Calories	700.7
Total Fat	41.3 g
Cholesterol	0 mg
Total Carbohydrate	69.7 g
Dietary Fiber	12.8 g
Protein	21.7 g

52. Peanut Butter Hummus

This kid-friendly recipe tastes really good. If you have children with sensitive tastes, this peanut butter hummus is highly recommended. You can use peanut butter instead of tahini- it still contains the nutrients that are present in the basic hummus. Perfect with crackers, pita wedges and just about any bread.

INGREDIENTS:

1 pinch paprika
1 tbsp. olive oil
1 tsp. minced fresh parsley
1 tsp. salt
1/3 c. natural creamy peanut butter
1/4 c. lemon juice
2 c. canned garbanzo beans
2 garlic cloves, halved

INSTRUCTIONS:

•Place all the ingredients in a food processor or blender.
•Process until the mixture becomes smooth and creamy. In case it is too thick, you can add water little by little until it achieves the needed consistency.
•Transfer in the serving bowl and drizzle some olive oil and sprinkle with parsley and paprika.

NUTRITIONAL VALUE:

Calories	61
Total Fat	3.1 g
Cholesterol	0 mg
Total Carbohydrate	6.6 g
Dietary Fiber	1.3 g
Protein	2.3 g

53. Hot Spinach Hummus

You will normally find this dip on the streets of Israel. It is simple and easy to make. You can change the amount of the ingredients if you want to make it even more flavorful. Some may prefer a stronger lemon taste, so instead of adding more water, you can increase the amount of lemon.

INGREDIENTS:

1 tsp. hot sauce (Tabasco)
⅓ c. lemon juice
⅓ c. tahini
⅓ c. water
¼ c. dried spinach (optional)
2 (15 oz.) cans chickpeas
2 garlic cloves, minced
2 tbsp. ground cumin
2 tsp. kosher salt
3 -4 tbsp. olive oil
paprika (optional)

INSTRUCTIONS:

•Drain and rinse the chickpeas.
•Place the tahini, lemon juice, olive oil, chickpeas, garlic, cumin, hot sauce and salt in the food processor or blender.
•Process, add more water and lemon juice as needed until the mixture achieves the needed consistency.
•Once you achieve the desired consistency, add spinach flakes and then pulse again until well blended.
•Transfer the mixture in a serving bowl, drizzle with olive oil and sprinkle some paprika.

NUTRITIONAL VALUE:

Calories	158.2
Total Fat	7.6 g
Cholesterol	0 mg
Total Carbohydrate	18.8 g
Dietary Fiber	3.9 g
Protein	4.9 g

54. Hummus with Cuban Black Beans

This is a delicious and easy to prepare recipe that many would surely love. This recipe was taken from an old Cuban recipe book and was handed down from generation to generation. Cuban black bean hummus is perfect together with warm pita, toasted baguette rounds and fresh veggie dippers.

INGREDIENTS:

1 (16 oz.) can Cuban black beans, drained
1 lime, juice of
1 tbsp. tahini
1 tsp. cumin
2 garlic cloves, peeled and sliced
3 tbsp. olive oil (Spanish for a Cuban taste)
Ground pepper, to taste
Salt, to taste

INSTRUCTIONS:

•Place all the ingredients in the food processor or blender. Process until the mixture becomes smooth and creamy.
•Transfer in an air tight container and refrigerate until it is time to serve. It will last up to a week in the refrigerator.
•Before serving let it stand for several minutes outside the ref.
•Serve together with pita, fresh veggies slices or sticks or baguette rounds.

NUTRITIONAL VALUE:

Calories	226
Total Fat	12.5 g
Cholesterol	0 mg
Total Carbohydrate	22.1 g
Dietary Fiber	7.6 g
Protein	8.2 g

55. Cumin in Light Sour Cream Hummus

This hummus recipe is without tahini and uses cumin instead. As compared to the basic hummus, this one is made of cumin and light sour cream. It tastes really creamy and yummy. If you are a big fan of hummus you should try this.

INGREDIENTS:

1 (15 oz.) can garbanzo beans
1 minced garlic clove
1 tbsp. olive oil
¼-½ tsp. cumin
2 tbsp. lemon juice
3 tbsp. light sour cream
Assorted fresh vegetable
Baby carrots
Pita chips
Salt and pepper

INSTRUCTIONS:

•Drain and rinse the chickpeas or garbanzo beans.
•Place chickpeas into a bowl and then add the garlic. Mash well, but still retain some texture.
•Add in the sour cream, lemon juice and olive oil.
•Add salt, pepper and cumin to taste.
•Serve together with carrots and other fresh vegetables or pita chips.

NUTRITIONAL VALUE:

Calories	87.3
Total Fat	2.9 g
Cholesterol	1.9 mg
Total Carbohydrate	12.9 g
Dietary Fiber	2.4 g
Protein	2.9 g

56. Hemp Seed Hummus

This recipe is a quick and nutritious dip. Perfect with pita bread or crackers or as a spread for your sandwich. If you are having a hard time encouraging your children to eat veggies, this is the solution. You can keep it in the fridge for about a week.

INGREDIENTS:

1 tsp. ground cumin
1 clove minced garlic
1 tsp. salt
1 (15 oz.) can kidney beans, rinsed and drained
1 (15 oz.) can garbanzo beans, rinsed and drained
2 tbsp. hemp seed hearts
1/2 c. fresh lemon juice
1/2 c. tahini
1/4 c. olive oil

INSTRUCTIONS:

•Combine tahini and lemon juice together in a food processor or blender until the mixture becomes smooth and creamy.
•Add garlic, salt, olive oil and cumin. Process again until smooth and creamy.
•Add ¼ of the garbanzo beans and kidney beans at a time to the mixture. Process, scrape the sides after every addition.
•Add the hemp seed hearts in the mixture and then process again until well combined and smooth.
•Transfer in the serving bowl.

NUTRITIONAL VALUE:

Calories	169
Cholesterol	0mg
Total Carbohydrates	14g
Dietary Fiber	4.3g
Protein	5.4g

57. Pinto Beans with Wine Hummus

With this recipe sesame seeds, garlic and onions are browned in wine, then combined with pinto beans for an amazing hummus. Serve together with chips or veggies.

INGREDIENTS:

2 cloves peeled garlic
1 c. chopped onions
1 c. dry pinto beans
2 c. water
1/2 c. red wine
1/4 c. sesame seeds

INSTRUCTIONS:

•In a saucepan, combine pinto beans and water and boil for two minutes.
•Replace the lid's saucepan and let it sit for about an hour. Then boil it again, set the heat at medium-low, and then simmer for 45 minutes or until the pinto beans are tender.
•Combine red wine, garlic, onions, and sesame seeds in a small saucepan and boil. Set the heat to medium-low and then simmer and stir occasionally for five to ten minutes or until the wine has evaporated.
•Place bean- water mixture in a food processor and blend until smooth. Add the onion mixture and process until smooth.

NUTRITIONAL VALUE:

Calories	131
Total Fat	2.6g
Cholesterol	0mg
Total Carbohydrates	18.6g
Dietary Fiber	4.6g
Protein	6.2g

58. Hummus with Spiriluna Powder

This Mediterranean style hummus enriches the flavor of your traditional hummus recipe by adding smoked chipotle and roasted garlic, and added nutrition courtesy of fresh spirulina.

INGREDIENTS:

1 (15 oz.) can drained chickpeas (liquid reserved)
1 tbsp. spirulina powder
1 clove roasted garlic, or more to taste
1 pinch salt
1 pinch smoked chipotle chile powder
1/4 c. tahini
1/2 lemon, juiced
1/4 c. olive oil

INSTRUCTIONS:

•Combine olive oil, garlic, chickpeas, lemon juice, tahini, chipotle chili powder, salt and spiriluna powder in the food processor or blender and process until smooth.
•If the mixture is too thick, slowly add the reserved chickpea liquid until it achieves the desired consistency.
•Transfer in the serving bowl and serve. For leftovers, you can store it in the fridge and can last for a week.

NUTRITIONAL VALUE:

Calories	149
Total Fat	11.2g
Cholesterol	0mg
Total Carbohydrates	10.1g
Dietary Fiber	2.3g
Protein	3.5g

59. Smoky Roasted Horseradish Hummus

If you want something that you will really satisfy your taste, try out this refreshing roasted horseradish hummus. To kick up the taste, a hint of rosemary is added. Enjoy this tasty hummus together with pita chips.

INGREDIENTS:

½ tsp. Kosher Salt
¾ tsp. Ground Cumin
1 ½ tsp. fresh minced rosemary
15 oz. Garbanzo Beans, Reserve 2 Tablespoons of Juice
2 ½ tbsp. Extra-Virgin Olive Oil
2 Fresh minced garlic cloves
2 tbsp. prepared horseradish
3 tbsp. fresh lemon juice
3 tbsp. Tahini
Dash of Cayenne

INSTRUCTIONS:

•Pre-heat your oven to 400° degrees Fahrenheit. On a non-stick cookie sheet, place the garbanzo beans. Drizzle ½ tablespoon of olive oil over the beans. Sprinkle one teaspoon of rosemary and sea salt. Stir to combine. Cook for about 15 mins. until golden brown.
•Once done, remove from heat and allow it to cool down for few minutes.
•Place tahini, olive oil, cayenne, roasted chickpeas, tahini, lemon juice, garlic cloves, cumin and horseradish in a food processor or blender. Scrape any remaining rosemary and salt on the cookie sheet.
•If the mixture is too thick, add one to two tablespoon of garbanzo juice; pulse and then pulse again until completely mixed.
•Transfer in a serving bowl and sprinkle rosemary on top. Serve with pita chips.

NUTRITIONAL VALUE:

Calories	1080
Total fat	41g
Cholesterol	0
Total Carbohydrate	143g
Dietary fiber	39g
Protein	45g

60. Beetroot Hummus

The colorful and fun variation of the basic hummus is the beetroot hummus. This recipe is the best creative snack for your children, an appetizer, or even a crowd- pleasing dip during parties.

INGREDIENTS:

¼ c. (60g) Tahini
½ tsp. salt or more to taste
1 cup (240g) chickpeas
1 tsp. garlic powder
1-2 tbsp. lemon juice
3 cooked beets (150g, about 2" diameter each)

INSTRUCTIONS:

•Place all the ingredients in a blender or food processor and blend until smooth. You can add more lemon juice if you want a little stronger taste or if the mixture is too thick.
•Transfer in a serving bowl and serve together with your favorite chips. Enjoy.
•For leftover hummus , you can store it in the fridge up to four days.

NUTRITIONAL VALUE:

Calories	178
Carbohydrate	20.7 grams
Protein	6.2 grams
Fat	8.8 grams
Cholesterol	0 mg

61. Italian Parsley with Bland Oil Hummus

For those who prefer a creamy hummus that is green and looks good to eat, this recipe is for you. This recipe is the modified version of the basic tahini hummus. The Italian Parsley hummus must be prepared several hours before serving for best flavor. Use only dried parsley for this recipe.

INGREDIENTS

1 ½ c. cooked chickpeas, reserve liquid
1 dash paprika
1 tbsp. extra virgin olive oil
1 tbsp. fresh flat-leaf Italian parsley
¼ tsp. cumin powder, very lightly dry roasted
¼ tsp. salt, to taste
2 -3 garlic cloves, minced
2 -3 tbsp. fresh lemon juice
2 tbsp. bland oil
3 tbsp. tahini, preferably homemade

INSTRUCTIONS:

•Add in all the ingredients except for the reserved bean liquid, into a blender or food processor.
•Gradually add some bean liquid via feeding tube while the blender is still running.
•Process until the mixture becomes smooth and creamy. If in case the mixture is too thick you can add more bean liquid.
•Scrape down the sides of the blender or food processor. Taste the mixture- you can add more salt, or lemon juice, depending on your preference. Keep in mind that hummus should not be too lemony, not too pasty, because of the sesame seeds, or not too garlicky.
•Transfer the hummus in a serving bowl and drizzle some olive oil and add a sprinkle of sumac. Garnish with fresh parsley.
•Serve with fresh veggies, chips, baked pita and others.

NUTRITIONAL VALUE:

Calories	177.9
Total Fat	11.1 g
Cholesterol	0 mg
Total Carbohydrate	16.4 g
Dietary Fiber	3.5 g
Protein	4.5 g

62. Hummus with Kalamata Olive

This hummus with Kalamata olives tastes really good, especially on warm pita triangles, radishes, green onions, cucumbers or carrots. The combination of the basic hummus ingredients and kalamata olives is definitely a yummy Mediterranean dish.

INGREDIENTS:

1 1/2 c. garbanzo beans, rinsed and drained
1 small red bell pepper, seeded and sliced
1 tsp. cayenne (keep some for topping)
1 tsp. ground cumin (set aside 1/4 tsp. for topping)
1/4 c. fresh lemon juice
1/4 c. tahini
2 garlic cloves
2 tbsp. capers
3 tbsp. fresh parsley (save 1 tbsp. for topping)
3/4 c. kalamata olive
4 tbsp. olive oil (reserve 2 tbsp. for topping)

INSTRUCTIONS:

•Place all the ingredients in a blender or food processor and process. To achieve the right consistency, add enough cold water.
•Transfer the mixture onto a serving bowl and smoothen the top using the back of the spoon. Drizzle with the rest of the olive oil and sprinkle with the remaining parsley.
•Also, sprinkle cayenne and cumin in a star pattern and then serve together with veggies or warm pita.
•Serve!

NUTRITIONAL VALUE:

Calories	357.7
Total Fat	24.8 g
Cholesterol	0 mg
Total Carbohydrate	29.4 g
Dietary Fiber	7 g
Protein	8 g

63. Coriander and Carrot Hummus

This hummus recipe is getting popular not only because of the taste, but because of the health benefits you can get from this. The roasted carrots provide a distinct taste to hummus. The sweetness of carrot and slight caramelization of sugar through roasting can captivate your senses.

INGREDIENTS:

1 lemon, juice of
1 teaspoon chili flakes
2 teaspoon freshly ground coriander
2 teaspoon peanut butter
3 cloves of garlic
300g peeled and chopped carrots (1 and ½ cups)
4 tablespoon olive oil
A small handful of fresh coriander
Pepper
Salt

INSTRUCTIONS:

•Roast the garlic cloves and carrots into the roasting tin, season and drizzle with olive oil and roast for twenty to thirty minutes until it starts to brown.
•While waiting for the carrots and garlic to roast, toast the coriander seeds before bashing them. Remove the roasted garlic skins.
•Place everything in a food processor or blender, adding olive oil 1 tablespoon at a time until it becomes smooth.
•Transfer in the serving bowl and serve together with pita breads.

NUTRITIONAL VALUE:

Calories	190
Total fat	15g
Cholesterol	0
Total Carbohydrate	14g
Protein	2g

64. Yummy Dilled Hummus

This dilled hummus is very interesting; you can try this version of hummus if you want something new. Perfect with pita chips, fresh veggies and others.

INGREDIENTS:

1 (15 oz.) can chickpeas, rinsed and drained
1 dash ground red pepper
1 tbsp. olive oil
1/4 c. tahini
1/4 tsp. salt
2 cloves minced garlic
2 tsp. snipped fresh dill or 1/2 tsp. dried dill
3 tbsp. lemon juice

INSTRUCTIONS:

•Combine chickpeas, tahini, lemon juice, garlic, sesame oil, salt, pepper and dill.
•Process until the mixture becomes smooth and creamy; stop and scrape the sides if needed.
•Pour in a serving bowl and serve. For leftovers, you can store it in an air tight container and refrigerate for up to one week.

NUTRITIONAL VALUE:

Calories	659.5
Total Fat	31.5 g
Cholesterol	0 mg
Total Carbohydrate	78.7 g
Dietary Fiber	16.5 g
Protein	21.6 g

65. Hummus with Chipotle Peppers

If you are a hummus lover but want to try other versions of this recipe, you can try this one. Hummus with chipotle peppers, together with cumin, is a bit spicy and smoky. Cilantro is added to brighten up the dish. This is perfect as a dip for chips and veggies during parties.

INGREDIENTS:

1 (7 oz.) jar roasted red peppers, drained
1 1/2 tsp. ground cumin
1 can whole chipotle pepper in Adobo sauce
1/2 c. roughly chopped fresh cilantro
1/2 c. water
1/2 tsp. salt
1/4 c. tahini
2 (15 oz.) cans chickpeas, drained
2 large garlic cloves
2 tbsp. olive oil
4 tbsp. fresh lemon juice
6 sun-dried tomatoes packed in oil
Fresh ground black pepper

INSTRUCTIONS:

•Place chickpeas, cumin, chipotle pepper, water, tahini, garlic, and olive oil in a food processor or blender and process until smooth and creamy.
•Add sun-dried tomatoes, salt, ground black pepper, red peppers and cilantro in the blender and then process again until smooth.
•Transfer the mixture to a serving bowl. Refrigerate and chill until it is time to serve.
•Before serving, bring the hummus to room temperature.
•Serve with warm pita chips.

NUTRITIONAL VALUE:

Calories	71.2
Fat	2.9 g
Cholesterol	0 mg
Total Carbohydrate	9.6 g
Dietary Fiber	2 g
Protein	2.4 g

66. Hummus with Pesto Sauce

If you want an Italian tasting hummus, this recipe is what you are looking for. Pesto is a sauce that originates in Northern Italy, and contains basil, European pine nuts and crushed garlic with olive oil, Fiore Sardo and Parmigian-Reggiano. This sauce will bring a summery taste to all types of dishes including hummus. This recipe uses a ready-made pesto sauce.

INGREDIENTS:

1 (19 oz.) can chickpeas, rinse & drain
1 garlic clove, minced
½ tsp. salt
⅓ c. prepared pesto sauce
¼ tsp. ground black pepper

INSTRUCTIONS:

•Place all the ingredients in a blender or food processor. Process until the mixture becomes smooth.
•Transfer the hummus in a serving container.
•Serve with breadsticks or hearty crackers.

NUTRITIONAL VALUE:

Calories	32.4
Total Fat	0.3 g
Cholesterol	0 mg
Total Carbohydrate	6.2 g
Dietary Fiber	1.2 g
Protein	1.4 g

67. Hummus with Plain Yogurt and Almonds

This is a Greek recipe that is simple, healthy and very tasty. Hummus is a very healthy dip and with the addition of almonds it makes the dip even healthier. The dip is easy to prepare, so if you need a dip for any occasion with limited time to prepare, this version of hummus is a good one.

INGREDIENTS:

1 (15 oz.) can chickpeas, drained
1 clove garlic, crushed
1 tbsp. olive oil
½ lemon,(juice of) to taste
¼ c. ground almonds
2 tsp. chopped of fresh mint
2 tsp. cumin seeds
2⁄3 c. regular plain yogurt
Cayenne pepper, to garnish (optional)
Olive oil, to garnish (optional)
Pita bread, cut into wedges
Salt & freshly ground black pepper, to taste

INSTRUCTIONS:

•In a small skillet, roast cumin seeds until aromatic.
•Set aside a few cumin seeds for garnish.
•Add cumin seeds in a blender or food processor together with garlic, lemon juice, chickpeas, pepper, ground almonds, olive oil, salt, mint and yogurt.
•Process until the mixture becomes smooth or to your desired consistency.
•Pour the hummus in a serving dish and let it stand for 30 mins.
•Drizzle some olive oil and sprinkle cumin seeds and cayenne pepper.
•Serve with pita chips or pita bread wedges.

NUTRITIONAL VALUE:

Calories	148.4
Total Fat	6.1 g
Cholesterol	3.5 mg
Total Carbohydrate	19 g
Dietary Fiber	3.7 g
Protein	5.5 g

68. Chocolate Hummus

This fiber and protein rich hummus recipe can be served for breakfast with your toast. You can use dark chocolate or any other type of chocolate to achieve the sweetness that you want for your hummus.

INGREDIENTS:

1 (15 oz.) can chickpeas
1 tsp. instant coffee powder (optional)
1 tsp. vanilla extract
½ c. Dutch-processed cocoa powder
½ c. granulated sugar
½ tsp. salt
3 oz. peanut butter
3 tbsp. olive oil
8 tbsp. water

INSTRUCTIONS:

•Place everything in a blender or food processor except the water. Scrape down any hummus sticking on the sides and continue mixing until well blended.
•While the motor is still running, add the water gradually; check the consistency before adding more.
•Serve with fresh fruits or toast.

NUTRITIONAL VALUE:

Calories	155.1
Total Fat	7.8 g
Cholesterol	0 mg
Total Carbohydrate	19.8 g
Dietary Fiber	3.2 g
Protein	4.2 g

69. Hummus with Macadamia Nuts

You can use this Hawaiian style hummus as a spread on your sliced bread, or as a dip for fresh raw veggies. This version of hummus uses macadamia nuts instead of tahini to make it taste even better.

INGREDIENTS:

1 tbsp. lemon juice
1 tsp. minced garlic
½ c. roasted macadamia nuts
10 medium basil leaves
2 c. garbanzo beans, drained
2 tbsp. olive oil
3 tbsp. water
Salt and pepper, to taste

INSTRUCTIONS:

•In a food processor bowl or blender, add all the ingredients and process until smooth.
•Transfer to a serving bowl and serve as dip for fresh veggies or as a spread on thinly sliced bread.

NUTRITIONAL VALUE:

Calories	163
Total Fat	10.4 g
Cholesterol	0 mg
Total Carbohydrate	15 g
Dietary Fiber	3.4 g
Protein	3.8 g

70. Hummus with Plain Yogurt and Cinnamon

Hummus lovers should try this traditional hummus with a twist of Moroccan cuisine and tomato. This recipe is prepared in a different way. To make it even tastier the ingredients were heated before blending it together. If stored in the fridge, it can last up to one week.

INGREDIENTS:

1 ½ tsp. lemon juice
1 small chopped onion
1 tsp. ground cumin
1 tsp. vegetable oil
540 ml chickpeas, drained (18oz. can)
½ c. plain yogurt
½ tsp. ground coriander
¼ tsp. cinnamon
⅛ tsp. cayenne
2 chopped garlic cloves
2 tbsp. tomato paste
Colorful veggies such as cucumbers, carrot, asparagus and peppers, cut into strips

INSTRUCTIONS:

Heat a large pan on medium heat. Add the oil and sauté the onion until soft or for about three minutes. Add the garlic and other spices. Stir until aromatic or for two minutes.
•Add the chickpeas and tomato paste. Allow the mixture to cool down.
•Place the chickpea mixture together with lemon juice and yogurt in a blender or food processor and process until smooth.
•Transfer the hummus into Mason jar about ¼ cup dip. Place the fresh veggies into the tip.

NUTRITIONAL VALUE:

Calories	420
Total Fat	7.8 g
Cholesterol	8 mg
Total Carbohydrate	73 g
Dietary Fiber	13.8 g
Protein	17.2 g

71. Yummy Beanless Zucchini Hummus

If you love hummus but your tummy is bean-sensitive, then this recipe is for you. This beanless zucchini hummus has authentic taste. If it is your first time to taste this recipe you won't notice that it does not contain any beans.

INGREDIENTS:

1 c. sunflower or sesame seeds, soaked
1 teaspoon turmeric
1/2 c. raw tahini
1/2 teaspoon ground cumin
2 pinches ground cayenne pepper
2 teaspoon paprika
2 teaspoon sea salt
3 raw peeled and chopped zucchini
4 cloves garlic
6 tablespoon lemon juice
Fresh parsley, minced for garnish
Extra-virgin olive oil, for drizzle

INSTRUCTIONS:

•Add all the ingredients, except parsley and oil, into food processor or blender and process until you achieve your desired consistency.
•Transfer hummus in a serving bowl and drizzle with extra-virgin olive oil and garnish with minced fresh parsley.
•Serve it with raw flax crackers, whole-grain pita bread or crudités. You can also use it as spread on sandwiches or as dressing for salad.

NUTRITIONAL VALUE:

Calories	140
Total Fat	11 g
Total Carbohydrate	8 g
Fiber	2 g
Protein	5 g
Cholesterol	0 mg

72. Hummus with Fresh Basil

If you love hummus and you want to add something into it to make it taste extra good, why not try adding fresh basil. This version of hummus is more healthy, tastes even better than the basic hummus and is easy to prepare.

INGREDIENTS:

1 tsp. salt
1⁄2 c. fresh basil
2 garlic cloves
2 tbsp. water
30 oz. cooked garbanzo beans
4 tbsp. extra virgin olive oil
4 tbsp. lemon juice
4 tbsp. tahini

INSTRUCTIONS:

•Place all the ingredients in a food processor or blender except for the salt and beans, and then process until smooth.
•Add salt and beans and then continue mixing. Taste and if needed, add more salt and process again until the mixture achieves the needed consistency.
•Serve with veggie sticks or chips.

NUTRITIONAL VALUE:

Calories	185.9
Total Fat	9.3 g
Cholesterol	0 mg
Total Carbohydrate	21.5 g
Dietary Fiber	4.4 g
Protein	5.4 g

73. Healthy Raw Nut Pulp Hummus

This hummus version is not just tasty, it is also very healthy. This recipe uses hazelnuts. Since nuts differ in tastes, you may need to adjust the seasonings that will best suit you.

INGREDIENTS:

1 ¼ c. hazelnut pulp
1 fat clove garlic
4 tablespoons lemon juice
2 tablespoons water
4 tablespoons raw tahini
1 teaspoon ground cumin
¼ teaspoon crushed chilies
pinch sea salt + pepper

INSTRUCTIONS:

•Combine minced garlic in a food processor and process. Add the other ingredients except for nut pulp and process until smooth.
•With the processor still running, add the nut pulp gradually, one spoonful at a time, until everything is well mixed.
•Add more water if needed, one tablespoon at a time, until the hummus achieves the desired consistency.
•Transfer in a serving bowl and store the leftovers in an airtight container in the refrigerator.

NUTRITIONAL VALUE:

Calories	360
Total fat	31g
Cholesterol	0mg
Total Carbohydrate	15g
Protein	13g
Dietary fiber	8g

74. Eggplant Hummus

This Middle Eastern dip and spread is similar to the basic hummus, but uses eggplant instead of garbanzo beans. This recipe features roasted eggplant as the main ingredient, which adds a smoky flavor that is delicious.

INGREDIENTS:

1 large eggplant
½ c. parsley, minced
½ tsp. black pepper
½ tsp. ground coriander
½ tsp. ground cumin
⅛ tsp. cayenne
4 peeled garlic cloves
Salt

INSTRUCTIONS:

•Pre-heat your oven to 375 degrees Fahrenheit. Create holes in eggplant using a fork.
•Cook for 45 mins.- allow it to cool down, then take the peel off.
•Combine garlic, coriander, eggplant, parsley, salt, cayenne, cumin and black pepper in your food processor or blender. Pulse until you reached the needed consistency.
•Serve cold with sliced pita bread or toasted flat bread triangles.

NUTRITIONAL VALUE: (For 2-3 cups of hummus)

Calories	656.4
Total Fat	6.4 g
Cholesterol	0 mg
Total Carbohydrate	128 g
Dietary Fiber	31.5 g
Protein	27.6 g

75. Vegan Friendly Harissa Hummus

This recipe is made with tahini paste, harissa, lemon juice, and with white beans. This vegan friendly hummus is very easy to prepare- all you need is a good quality food processor or blender. All natural harissa is readily available in the market.

INGREDIENTS:

¼ cup fresh lemon juice
¼ cup tahini paste
1 15.5 ounce can of low salt white beans
1 clove garlic
1 tablespoon harissa, plus more, if you want a spicy hummus
1 teaspoon kosher salt
Extra harissa for garnish

INSTRUCTIONS:

•Combine all the ingredients in a food processor or blender. Process several times and then pulse at medium speed until well mixed.
•Transfer in a serving bowl and garnish it with harissa. Serve with your favorite chips or crackers.

NUTRITIONAL VALUE:

Calories	208
Total Fat	10g
Total Carbohydrates	23g
Protein	9g

76. Hummus with Black Tea and Raspberry Jam

This hummus recipe is a dessert and it tastes really good. It provides you all the classic flavors but this is much better. If you want something sweet, but at the same time, a little bit spicy, try this recipe.

INGREDIENTS:

½ c. natural-style peanut butter
2 tbsp. raspberry jam
¾ c. garbanzo beans , cooked and drained
¾ c. red kidney beans, cooked and drained
8 tsp. black tea

INSTRUCTIONS:

•Combine all the ingredients, except for the jam, in your blender or food processor and process until smooth and creamy.
•You might need to add more or less liquid, depending on the beans that you will use.
•Add in the jam and store in the refrigerator until it is time to serve. This is perfect with cookies and fruits.

NUTRITIONAL VALUE:

Calories	626.4
Total Fat	33.9 g
Cholesterol	0 mg
Total Carbohydrate	61.9 g
Dietary Fiber	13 g
Protein	26.5 g

77. Hummus with Low Fat Sour Cream and Parmesan Cheese

This recipe is so versatile. It is great as a healthy snack with warm pita bread, veggies or crackers. You may also use this as a spread for your pita sandwiches and quesadillas. It only takes a few minutes to whip the ingredients together.

INGREDIENTS:

1 can chickpeas, drained and rinsed (liquid reserved)
2 tablespoons Tahini
2 tablespoons freshly squeezed lemon juice
2 teaspoons minced garlic
1 teaspoon liquid honey
2 tablespoons grated parmesan cheese
1/2 c. Low Fat Sour Cream
1/2 teaspoon sesame oil
1/4 teaspoon ground coriander
1/8 teaspoon ground cumin

INSTRUCTIONS:

•Add in all the ingredients in a food processor or blender and process until smooth.
•If the mixture is too thick, you can add the reserved bean liquid, one tablespoon at a time, until you reached the needed consistency.
•Transfer in an air tight container and refrigerate.
•Serve with crackers, warm pita wedges or fresh veggies.

NUTRITIONAL VALUE:

Calories	135.8
Total Fat	3.6 g
Cholesterol	2.4 mg
Total Carbs:	20.7 g
Dietary Fiber	4.0 g
Protein	6.1 g

78. Hummus with Chipotle Chile and Orange

This recipe is not just smooth and yummy, but very healthy as well, with the addition of refreshing orange juice and zest and chipotle in adobo sauce. Perfect with toasted pitas, as a spread in wraps and spread on toasted rye crackers topped with tomatoes. You may also add diced red roasted peppers.

INGREDIENTS:

1 chipotle chile in adobo, remove the seed if you prefer less heat
1 orange, juice and zest of
1 pinch smoked paprika (garnish)
1 tbsp. olive oil, adding more if desired
1 tsp. fresh parsley or 1 tsp. minced fresh cilantro (garnish)
1/3 c. tahini
2 -4 minced garlic cloves
2 c. chickpeas, rinsed and drained

INSTRUCTIONS:

•In a food processor, place all the ingredients, except for the zest. Process until smooth and creamy.
•Add more olive oil via feed tube over the chickpeas mixture to produce a smooth hummus if required.
•Taste- you can add zest if more orange flavor is needed.
•Transfer hummus in a serving bowl. Drizzle with olive oil and sprinkle with parsley, paprika or cilantro.

NUTRITIONAL VALUE:

Calories	78.5
Total Fat	3.6 g
Cholesterol	0 mg
Total Carbohydrate	9.8 g
Dietary Fiber	2.2 g
Protein	2.5 g

79. Hummus with Tamarind and Fresh Ginger

African cuisines are on the top in making delectable and unique tamarind recipes. Tamarind is native to Africa and grows wild throughout the Sudan where there is Arabian influence in their cuisine. This is also served in the Arabian Gulf as a meze. It has a very tasty flavour from the tart tamarind.

INGREDIENTS:

1 ½ tbsp. finely chopped fresh ginger
1 tbsp. cilantro leaves or 1 tbsp. flat leaf parsley
1 tbsp. extra virgin olive oil
2 c. canned chick-peas, rinsed
2 tbsp. tamarind paste
3 tbsp. tahini
Fresh ground black pepper
Fresh lemon juice, to taste
Minced garlic, to taste
Sea salt
Water

INSTRUCTIONS:

•Add all the ingredients, except for parsley, olive oil and coriander, in a blender or food processor and process to make a thick paste- add more water if needed.
•Taste and you can add salt if needed.
•Transfer to a serving bowl and sprinkle with chopped parsley or coriander and extra virgin olive oil before serving.

NUTRITIONAL VALUE:

Calories	247.6
Total Fat	10.2 g
Cholesterol	0 mg
Total Carbohydrate	32.8 g
Dietary Fiber	6.6 g
Protein	8.1 g

80. Hummus with Sprouted Raw Nut

For those who need food fast, this easy to prepare hummus is the answer. You can make different variations on this recipe, and also various ways to use it. This hummus variation with sprouted raw nut is an excellent sour of alkalizing protein, heart healthy fats, minerals, enzymes, antioxidant rich carbs, and vitamins, which makes it a perfect food for replenishing your energy after working out.

INGREDIENTS:

1 c. raw almonds (soak overnight, then drain and rinse)
1 c. cashews (soak overnight, then drain and rinse)
1 to 2 tsp. fresh garlic
½ c. chopped onion
¼ to ⅓ c. raw tahini
1 tsp. ground cumin
⅓ to ½ c. fresh lemon juice, or to taste
¼ to ⅓ c. extra virgin olive oil
½ tsp. fine sea salt or to taste
½ tsp. freshly ground pepper or to taste
Fresh chopped herbs, cayenne pepper, and lemon zest (garnish)

INSTRUCTIONS:

•Place raw almonds, cashews, onion and fresh garlic in a food processor then add the cumin, lemon juice and tahini.
•Process to combine and while the processor is running slowly add olive oil. Add more lemon juice and olive oil to adjust the consistency. You need a very thick hummus if used in wraps like nori leaves.
•Adjust seasonings and taste if needed.
•Transfer in the serving bowl and drizzle additional olive oil, sprinkle some nut,

lemon zest, and paprika or cayenne pepper.
•If used as spread for wraps, chill for one hour and then spread a 2 inch wide and ½ inch thick layer of hummus.

NUTRITIONAL VALUE:

Calories	289
Total fat	21.2g
Cholesterol	0mg
Total carbohydrate	11g
Dietary fiber	7g
Protein	7.89g

81.Hummus with Tamari and Curry Powder

If you have tried different versions of hummus and you want something new, you can try this Tamari with curry powder hummus. It is easy to prepare and at the same time tastes better than the basic hummus. Also, you can make this hummus a little bit chunky by adding toasted sesame seeds. This recipe does not contain olive oil.

INGREDIENTS:

1 -2 tbsp. tamari
1 medium chopped onion
1 tbsp. curry powder
½ c. chopped fresh parsley
¼ c. tahini
¼ c. toasted sesame seeds
2 (10 oz.) cans chickpeas, drained and rinsed
2 cloves minced garlic
2 tbsp. cider vinegar
2 tbsp. fresh lemon juice
Salt and pepper

INSTRUCTIONS:

•Combine onion, vinegar, curry powder, lemon juice, tamari and garlic in a food processor and process until smooth.
•Add ½ of the chickpeas and ½ of the tahini and then blend again until smooth.
•Add the rest of the tahini and chickpeas and blend coarsely, so the mixture is a little bit chunky.
•Over medium heat, toast the sesame seeds in a heavy skillet until golden brown. To avoid burning, stir constantly or shake the pan.
•Add parsley and sesame seeds to the hummus and stir to mix. Add the seasoning to taste.
•You can use this hummus as a filling for your sandwich, a dip for your fresh veggies or toasted pita wedges.

NUTRITIONAL VALUE:

Calories	204.8
Total Fat	9.1 g
Cholesterol	0 mg
Total Carbohydrate	25.4 g
Dietary Fiber	5.9 g
Protein	7.6 g

82. Hummus with Wasabi

If you want an extra spicy flavor for your dip, this wasabi hummus will really make you hot. This hummus tastes good with veggies, chips and on wraps or sandwiches. You can adjust the amount of wasabi depending on how hot you want your hummus.

INGREDIENTS:

1 inch fresh ginger or 2 tsp. dried
1 tablespoon lemon juice
1 tablespoon olive oil
1 tablespoon soy sauce (gluten free is needed)
15 ounce can garbanzo beans, rinsed and drained
2 tablespoon tahini
2 tablespoon water or more if needed
2-4 teaspoon wasabi
Salt and pepper to taste

INSTRUCTIONS:

•Add all the ingredients in a blender or food processor and process until smooth.
•In case the mixture is too thick, add more water. Serve with oven baked pita chips, fresh veggies or on wraps and sandwiches.

NUTRITIONAL VALUE:

Calories	480
Cholesterol	0
Total Carbohydrate	70g
Dietary Fiber	20g
Protein	22g

83. Tasty Broccoli Hummus

If you want to get more veggies in your diet, this tasty broccoli hummus recipe is the best way to do that, and is a better variation from traditional hummus. Using broccoli in hummus, you make the dish even healthier. Dip your fresh veggies in your broccoli hummus and you get more veggies in your diet.

INGREDIENTS:

½ c. sour cream
1 15-oz. can cannellini beans, rinsed and drained
1 large green onion
1 tbsp. fresh lemon juice
12-oz. bag of fresh broccoli, steamed
2 small peeled cloves of garlic
3-4 tbsp. olive oil
Salt and pepper to taste
Small handful fresh parsley

INSTRUCTIONS:

•Place the cooked broccoli, parsley, lemon juice and green onion in your blender or food processor and blend until completely broken down.
•Add in the olive oil, beans, and sour cream and blend until smooth. If the mixture is too thick you can add more water, one tablespoon at a time.
•Taste and add pepper and salt.

NUTRITIONAL VALUE:

Calories	570
Total Fat	21g
Cholesterol	10mg
Total Carbohydrate	75g
Dietary Fiber	29g
Protein	27g

84. Hummus with Lima Beans

This hummus recipe is different because it is uses lima beans instead of garbanzo beans. Just like any other hummus recipe, lima bean hummus is easy to prepare. The preparation will only take around 5 to 10 mins. You can use it as dip or spread.

INGREDIENTS:

1 c. olive oil
1 pound dried butter beans (Lima beans)
½ tsp. cayenne
½ tsp. freshly ground black pepper
⅓ c. tahini
¼ c. freshly squeezed lemon juice
2 tsp. kosher salt
4 garlic cloves

INSTRUCTIONS:

•Prepare the lima beans. Soak the lima beans overnight. Drain and discard the water.
•Pour water in a medium size pot and add the lima beans- bring to boil and then simmer until they are soft or tender. Do not overcook. Drain the beans and reserve the cooking liquid.
•In a food processor, add the beans, cayenne, garlic, salt, tahini and pepper. Puree the mixture; with the processor still running, pour the lemon juice and olive oil slowly.
•In case the mixture is too thick, add the reserved cooking liquid, one tablespoon at a time, until it becomes smooth and creamy.
•Taste- you can add more cayenne and salt if needed.

NUTRITIONAL VALUE:

Calories	1312.7
Total Fat	85.9 g
Cholesterol	0 mg
Total Carbohydrate	106.4 g
Dietary Fiber	31.6 g
Protein	37.6 g

85. Hummus with Sambal Oelek and Butter Beans

This protein rich hummus recipe is very delicious. If you want it extra creamy use homemade tahini. For those who like a spicy hummus, you should try this recipe. This dip is best with fresh veggies and pita chips. (Sambal oelek is a spicy southeast Asian chile sauce made from hot chile peppers, salt, and sometimes vinegar)

INGREDIENTS:

1 (15 oz.) can butter beans
1 (15 oz.) can chickpeas, drained and rinsed
1 tsp. sambal oelek
1/2 lemon, juice of
2 cloves minced garlic
2 tbsp. tahini
3 tbsp. extra virgin olive oil
3 tbsp. plain low-fat yogurt
5 tbsp. water
fresh ground black pepper, to taste
sea salt, to taste

INSTRUCTIONS:

•Place all the ingredients in a blender or food processor, except for pepper and salt, and process until smooth and creamy.
•Add pepper and salt to taste.
•In case the mixture is too thick, add more water, one tablespoon at a time, until you achieved the right consistency.

NUTRITIONAL VALUE:

Calories	230
Total Fat	10.3 g
Cholesterol	0.4 mg
Total Carbohydrate	28 g
Dietary Fiber	6.2 g
Protein	7.8 g

86. Hummus with Black Olives and Beans

Delicious dip for pita wedges, chunks of grainy bread or veggies. Although, it may contain additional ingredients like black olives, some still consider this as the real hummus. This hummus recipe is very easy to prepare with lots of healthy benefits.

INGREDIENTS:

1 (15 oz.) can black beans, drain and reserve liquid
1 ½ tbsp. tahini
1 clove garlic
½ tsp. salt
¼ tsp. cayenne pepper
¼ tsp. paprika
10 chopped black olives
2 tbsp. lemon juice
¾ tsp. ground cumin

INSTRUCTIONS:

•Place the garlic in the food processor and process. Add 2 tbsp. of reserved liquid, the black beans, tahini, 2 tbsp. lemon juice, 1/8 tsp. cayenne pepper, ½ tsp cumin, and ½ tsp. salt.
•Process until smoot- scrape the sides of the food processor bowl if needed.
•Add the remaining seasonings and liquids to taste.
•Garnish with chopped black olives and paprika.
•Serve together with your favorite veggies, chunks of grainy bread or toasted pita wedges.

NUTRITIONAL VALUE:

Calories	75.6
Total Fat	2.2 g
Cholesterol	0 mg
Total Carbohydrate	10.8 g
Dietary Fiber	3.9 g
Protein	4 g

87. Hummus with Serrano Peppers and Cilantro

This hummus recipe is a combination of Latin American and Mediterranean flavors. This recipe tastes so delicious that you don't have to buy one in the supermarket. You can make more than one serving if you have plans of including it in your snack or lunch in the coming days. You can use this as a dip for your favorite crackers or as a spread on your pita sandwiches. You can even use it as stuffing for your chicken breast.

INGREDIENTS:

1 (15 oz.) can black beans, drained
1 (15 oz.) can chickpeas, drained
1/3 c. cilantro, minced
1/3 c. olive oil
2 -4 serrano peppers, seeded and minced
2 limes, juice of
2 tbsp. tahini
2 tsp. ground cumin
4 -5 minced garlic cloves
salt and pepper (to taste)

INSTRUCTIONS:

•Place the black beans, tahini, lime juice, chickpeas, olive oil, garlic and cumin in a food processor or blender and process until smooth.
•Add cilantro, Serrano peppers, salt and pepper to taste and process.
•Transfer the hummus in serving bowl.
•Serve together with pita sandwiches or crackers.

NUTRITIONAL VALUE:

Calories	149.8
Total Fat	7.8 g
Cholesterol	0 mg
Total Carbohydrate	16.5 g
Dietary Fiber	4.4 g
Protein	4.7 g

88.Hummus with Vegetable Oil and Red Pepper Flakes

This hummus recipe is easy to prepare and very healthy. This will not only fill you up, but also warms you up. It is best served together with fresh lime wedges to kick up the flavor, and you can serve it over brown rice.

INGREDIENTS:

1 (14 1/2 oz.) can diced tomatoes
1 (14 1/2 oz.) can vegetable broth
1 lime
1 medium chopped onion
1 tbsp. vegetable oil
1 tsp. ground cumin
1⁄4-1⁄2 tsp. crushed red pepper flakes
2 (15 oz.) cans black beans, rinsed
2 minced garlic cloves
2 tsp. chili powder

INSTRUCTIONS:

•Heat oil in a three quart sauce pan over medium heat; sauté onion, stir occasionally until translucent and tender, or for about five to seven minutes.
•Add in the garlic and spices and sauté for another minute.
•Add in the broth, beans and tomatoes. If you want, you can add salt to taste.
•Boil the soup, reduce the heat and then simmer without covering for around 15 mins.
•Spoon 1/3 of the mixture and place into a food processor or blender and process until smooth- you can add more or less depending on how thick you want your hummus.

NUTRITIONAL VALUE:

Calories	284.5
Total Fat	4.8 g
Cholesterol	0 mg
Total Carbohydrate	48.9 g
Dietary Fiber	16.2 g
Protein	15.1 g

89. Green Olive, Spinach and Avocado Hummus

This hummus recipe is very healthy and also tastes better as compared to the traditional hummus. With the addition of avocado, the hummus becomes creamier and sweet. The olives add saltiness to balance the taste. To complete the taste and health benefits of the hummus, spinach is added.

INGREDIENTS:

1(15 oz. can) of Garbanzo Beans, drained (liquid reserved)
1/2 roughly chopped avocado
1 c. roughly chopped baby spinach
1 roughly chopped garlic clove
1 tbsp. Tahini
Green olives
Juice of 1 Lemon

INSTRUCTIONS:

•Place all the ingredients in a food processor or blender and process until smooth and creamy. Scrape the mixture sticking on the sides of the bowl.
•If the mixture is too thick, add the reserved bean liquid, one tablespoon at a time.
•Transfer the hummus in a serving bowl and serve together with pretzel thins, pita chips or raw veggies. You can also use it as spread for your tortilla wraps or sandwich bread.

NUTRITIONAL VALUE:

Calories	460
Total fat	12g
Cholesterol	0mg
Total Carbohydrates	72g
Dietary fiber	22g
Protein	22g

90. Hummus with Pine Nuts and Parsley

If you want to spice up your hummus and give the traditional recipe a twist, here is a good version of the dip. With this recipe the starchiness of the garbanzo beans is balanced by the sharpness of the parsley oil. Also the bright green oil provides the dip an appealing color.

INGREDIENTS:

1 tsp. cumin seed
1 tsp. salt
¼ c. packed fresh flat-leaf parsley
2 (19 oz.) cans garbanzo beans, drained and rinsed
⅔ c. water
⅔ c. well-stirred tahini
3 tbsp. pine nuts
¾ c. extra virgin olive oil
4 garlic cloves
5 tbsp. fresh lemon juice (to taste)

INSTRUCTIONS:

•Pre-heat your oven to 350 degrees Fahrenheit. Position the rack at the center of the oven.
•Toast the cumin seeds and pine nuts in a small skillet in the oven until brown, or for about 8 mins. Stir occasionally. Allow it to cool down.
•Combine ¼ cup olive oil with ¼ cup parsley in a blender or food processor. Then add ½ cup garbanzo beans and garlic and process until the mixture becomes smooth.
•Add water, salt, tahini, lemon juice, the rest of the garbanzo beans and the remaining olive oil, and process until creamy and smooth.
•Transfer the hummus in a serving bowl and drizzle with parsley oil and sprinkle cumin seeds and pine nuts on top.
•Serve best with pita toast.

NUTRITIONAL VALUE:

Calories	961.6
Total Fat	67.3 g
Cholesterol	0 mg
Total Carbohydrate	75.3 g
Dietary Fiber	16.1 g
Protein	21.8 g

91. Roasted Grape Tomatoes and Garlic Hummus

This roasted grape tomatoes and garlic hummus is very delicious. Roasting tomatoes and garlic will bring out the best of their flavors. Adding parmesan cheese will add depth into the recipe and the lemon juice will brighten the dip. This dip is perfect with toasted garlic bread or with your favorite veggies.

INGREDIENTS:

⅛ tsp. black pepper
⅔ cup. grated Parmesan cheese
1 (15-oz.) can unsalted garbanzo beans, rinsed and drained
1 tbsp. olive oil, divided
1 tsp. kosher salt, divided
2 c. grape tomatoes
2 garlic bulbs
2 tbsp. extra virgin olive oil
3 ½ tbsp. fresh squeezed lemon juice
3 tbsp. tahini
Basil, pine nuts, olive oil, and parmesan to garnish
Salt, pepper

INSTRUCTIONS:

•Pre-heat your oven to 400 degrees Fahrenheit.
•Toss two cups of tomatoes with ½ tsp salt and ½ tbsp. olive oil. Place garlic bulbs in foil- cut off the top ¼ inch down to expose and remove excess peel. On top of the garlic, drizzle ½ tbsp. of olive oil. Roast the garlic and tomatoes on a baking sheet. Tomatoes will be cooked first for about 20 mins.- remove it from the baking sheet and transfer it to a bowl .
•Cook the garlic for another 20 to 30 mins. until golden brown. Once done, squeeze the garlic to remove the cloves from bulb.
•Place the roasted tomatoes, grated Parmesan cheese, extra virgin olive oil, tahini, garbanzo beans, lemon juice, ½ tsp. salt and 1/8 tsp. pepper in a food processor.
•Process, scrape down the sides and process again until it achieves the needed consistency.
•Taste and adjust the salt and lemon juice to your taste.
•Serve and garnish with pine nuts, parmesan cheese, basil chiffonade, and olive oil.

NUTRITIONAL VALUE:

Calories	740
Total fat	38g
Cholesterol	15mg
Total Carbohydrate	75g
Dietary fiber	21g
Protein	32 g

92. Hummus with Red Lentils

This hummus recipe uses red lentils instead of chickpeas and it tastes yummy. To add color into it, turmeric can be added. You can also add some paprika if you prefer a red hummus. If you are looking for an easy to prepare lentil dish, this recipe is for you.

INGREDIENTS:

1 1/2-2 tbsp. fresh lemon juice
1 c. dried split red lentils
1 head roasted garlic
1 tbsp. tahini
2 tsp. cumin
Salt

INSTRUCTIONS:

•Prepare red lentils by boiling for 20 mins. or until tender.
•Completely drain the lentils.
•Place all the ingredients, including the lentils, in a blender or food processor. Process the mixture until smooth and creamy.
•Transfer in a serving bowl and serve together with your favorite pita chips or crackers.

NUTRITIONAL VALUE:

Calories	207.3
Total Fat	2.6 g
Cholesterol	0 mg
Total Carbohydrate	33.2 g
Dietary Fiber	15.3 g
Protein	13.7 g

93. Hummus with Light Cream Cheese

If you want a more spreadable hummus, light cream cheese is added to the original recipe of hummus. This will give the hummus a richer effect. This recipe is easy to prepare and healthy.

INGREDIENTS:

1 (15 oz.) can garbanzo beans
1 tbsp. light cream cheese
1 tbsp. minced garlic
1 tsp. lemon juice
1 tsp. olive oil
1 tsp. paprika
½ c. sesame seeds

INSTRUCTIONS:

•Combine beans, lemon juice, olive oil, sesame seeds, garlic, and cream cheese in a food processor or blender. Process the mixture until well combined and smooth.
•Transfer hummus in a serving bowl and sprinkle with paprika.
•Drizzle some olive oil to make it more appealing.

NUTRITIONAL VALUE:

Calories	253.8
Total Fat	12.2 g
Cholesterol	2.7 mg
Total Carbohydrate	29.5 g
Dietary Fiber	7 g
Protein	9 g

94. Hummus with Red Curry Paste and Coconut Milk

This recipe is very addictive. You might get into the habit of making hummus in a huge quantity once a week. The combination of creamy coconut milk, lime, chickpeas, garlic and red curry paste is perfect. You can top it with Thai basil if you want.

INGREDIENTS:

¾ c. unsweetened full-fat coconut milk
1 tsp. salt
1/3 c. red curry paste
2 – 15 oz. cans chickpeas, drained
3 garlic cloves
Garnish with fresh Thai basil leaves
Zest of 2 limes

INSTRUCTIONS:

•In a food processor, add the red curry paste, lime zest, chickpeas salt and garlic. Add ½ cup of coconut milk on top.
•Process until the mixture becomes very smooth, then check if it has the needed consistency. If in case the mixture is too thick, you can add another ¼ cup coconut milk and process again.
•Transfer the hummus in a serving bowl and sprinkle some chopped Thai basil on top.
•Serve with rice crackers or veggies.

NUTRITIONAL VALUE:

Calories	80
Total Fat	6 g
Total Carbs	7 g
Dietary Fiber	2 g
Sugars	1 g
Protein	2 g
Cholesterol	0 mg

95. Stimulating Walnut Hummus

A nutritious and delicious dip, appetizer or snack that is easy to make. This hummus recipe is tahini and olive oil free. To add zest into the dish, toasted walnuts are added.

INGREDIENTS:

1 (19 oz.) can chick peas, drained and rinsed (reserve liquid)
1/2 tsp. cayenne pepper
1/4 c. Italian salad dressing
1/2 c. toasted walnuts

INSTRUCTIONS:

•Place walnuts, cayenne pepper, chickpeas and salad dressing in a food processor or blender. Process until the mixture becomes smooth.
•If in case the mixture is too thick, add the reserved liquid, one tablespoon at a time, until the mixture reached the needed consistency.
•Transfer the hummus in a serving bowl and serve with pita triangles or vegetable sticks.

NUTRITIONAL VALUE:

Calories	68
Total Fat	3.4g
Cholesterol	0mg
Total Carbohydrates	7.6g
Dietary Fiber	1.6g
Protein	2g

96. Hummus with Honey and Sriracha

This honey and sriracha hummus recipe is a sweet and spicy combo. This recipe is very hot and is not for the faint of heart. This hummus recipe is slightly sweet and very velvety. This is a great recipe to serve as an appetizer with crackers or pita chips.

INGREDIENTS:

¼ c. olive oil
¼ c. Sriracha
½ tsp. sea salt
1 tsp. garlic powder
2 (14.5 oz.) cans garbanzo beans, drained & rinsed
2 tbsp. honey
3 tbsp. cold water

INSTRUCTIONS:

•Place garbanzo beans in a food processor or blender and process until smooth.
•Add in the olive oil, honey and sriracha and process again until well mixed and smooth.
•Scrape any mixture that might stick on the side of the processor.
•Add salt and garlic powder and process again. Taste- you can add more salt if needed.
•With the processor still running, add the water gradually through the lid. Continue blending until the mixture becomes creamy and smooth.
•Transfer the hummus in a serving bowl.

NUTRITIONAL VALUE:

Calories	50
Cholesterol	0mg
Total Carbohydrate	5g
Dietary Fiber	2g
Protein	2g

97. Hummus with Maple Syrup and Vanilla Extract

Vanilla extract and maple syrup in hummus makes this dip even better. The chickpeas will provide the nutty flavor, while maple and vanilla will provide the sweetness. Since the base of your dip is the chickpeas, this dip is a good source of protein, minerals and vitamins. This recipe is perfect as dip for strawberries, apples, bananas, or even on your graham crackers.

INGREDIENTS:

1 1/2 c. cooked garbanzo beans
1 tsp. ground cinnamon
1 tsp. vanilla extract
1/4 c. chocolate chips
2 tbsp. maple syrup
3 tbsp. nut or seed butter, such as peanut butter
4 tbsp. butter, at room temperature
large pinch sea salt

INSTRUCTIONS:

• In a food processor, place the garbanzo beans and process until crumbly.
• Add the other ingredients, except for the chocolate chips, in the food processor and
• process until the mixture is smooth.
• Transfer into a serving bowl. Place chocolate chips on top and serve.
• You can store leftovers in the ref and will last up to 3 days.

NUTRITIONAL VALUE:

Calories	150
Total Fat	3 grams
Total Carbohydrates	25 grams
Dietary Fiber	3.5 grams
Protein	3 grams
Cholesterol	0 mg

98. Humus with Miso

This miso hummus recipe is super tasty. It provides a new twist to the traditional hummus. If you are looking for a more flavorful dip, this recipe is a good one. Miso adds a certain unique flavor to your hummus.

INGREDIENTS:

1 (15.5 oz. / 439 g) can garbanzo beans, rinse and drained
1 fat garlic clove, peeled and crushed
2 tbsp. sweet white miso
2 tbsp. water, plus more as needed
Black pepper
Juice of half a lemon
Olive oil

INSTRUCTIONS:

•Place garbanzo beans, miso, garlic, 2 tablespoon of water and lemon juice in a food processor or blender. Process for a couple of minutes until the mixture becomes smooth and creamy.
•Add more water if needed, one tablespoon at a time, until you achieve a spreadable hummus.
•Transfer the mixture to a serving bowl, and garnish it with black pepper and olive oil.
•Serve with crudités, crackers, pita or breadsticks.

NUTRITIONAL VALUE:

Calories	470
Total Fat	12g
Cholesterol	0mg
Total Carbohydrate	73g
Dietary Fiber	20g
Protein	22g

99. Hummus with White Beans and Harissa

This vegan friendly easy-to-do hummus recipe is very yummy and at the same time easy to prepare. It will only take around five to ten minutes to prepare. Even the figure conscious individual can eat this without gaining additional weight.

INGREDIENTS:

¼ cup fresh lemon juice
¼ cup tahini paste
1 15.5 oz. can of low salt white beans
1 clove garlic
1 tablespoon harissa- if you want a spicier hummus you can add more
1 teaspoon kosher salt
Extra harissa for garnish

INSTRUCTIONS:

•Put all the ingredients in a food processor or blender. Process for a couple of minutes until the mixture becomes smooth and creamy.
•Transfer the hummus in a serving bowl and extra harissa can be added as garnish if desired.

NUTRITIONAL VALUE:

Calories	208
Carbohydrates	23g
Fat	10g
Protein	9g
Sodium	724mg
Sugar	1g

100. Hummus with Flaxseed

Flaxseed in hummus makes the dip thicker and yummy. This recipe still contains all the nutrients that the traditional has- the added ingredients simply makes it even more nutritious.

INGREDIENTS:

1 can (15.5 ounce) of chickpeas
1 tsp. of kosher salt
1/2 c. of olive oil
1/4 to 1/2 c. of cold water
2 cloves minced garlic
2 tbsp. of flaxseed
2 tbsp. of tahini
4 tbsp. of fresh lemon juice

INSTRUCTIONS:

•Place all the ingredients except for olive oil in a blender or food processor and process until well combined.
•Scrape down the sides of the food processor and then continue processing. Repeat this procedure two more times to ensure that everything is well incorporated until creamy and smooth.
•With the processor still running, slowly add the olive oil.
•Taste and add more seasoning if needed.
•Serve immediately or chilled.

NUTRITIONAL VALUE:

Calories	1380
Total Fat	74g
Cholesterol	0
Total Carbohydrate	142g
Dietary Fiber	39g
Protein	45g

Conclusion

Hummus, the easy-to-do dip of olive oil, salt, chickpeas and lemon juice, has taken America by storm. According to New York Times the hummus industry has grown fast, from only a five million dollar industry 15 years ago, to a total of $530 million in 2012. The variations and different versions of hummus recipes also increased. This savory, irresistible dip is very nutritious and delicious. There are lots of health benefits that you can get from eating hummus regularly.

For figure conscious individuals, this dip or spread will not only satisfy your palate, but will also help you in keeping your body fit and healthy. If you feel that you are too addicted with hummus, don't worry, you are not alone. There are lots of hummus lovers who make their own variation of hummus. The taste of your hummus will depend on what beans you used or the nuts. Some people may also experiment as to what ingredients will enhance the taste of the basic hummus. So, the next time you feel like having hummus dip at lunch, do not hesitate to do so. At present, it is considered as one of the healthiest foods that you can consume on a daily basis.

Hope this book was able to help you find the perfect variation of hummus for your favorite fruits, veggies, bread, crackers and pita.

Printed in Great Britain
by Amazon